William Lovett

LIVES of the LEFT is a new series of original biographies of leading figures in the European and North American socialist and labour movements. Short, lively and accessible, they will be welcomed by students of history and politics and by anyone interested in the development of the Left.   *general editor* David Howell

published: **J. Ramsay MacDonald** Austen Morgan
James Maxton William Knox
Karl Kautsky Dick Geary
'Big Bill' Haywood Melvyn Dubofsky
A. J. Cook Paul Davies
R. H. Tawney Anthony Wright
Thomas Johnston Graham Walker
Arthur Henderson Fred Leventhal
William Lovett Joel Wiener

forthcoming, to include: **John Strachey** Michael Newman
Tom Mann Joseph White
John MacLean Brian Ripley and John McHugh
Eugene Debs Gail Malmgreen

For Suzanne, Paul, Debbie and Jane

LIVES
of the
LEFT

William Lovett

Joel Wiener

Manchester University Press
Manchester and New York

Distributed exclusively in the USA and Canada by St. Martin's Press

Copyright © Joel Wiener 1989

Published by Manchester University Press, Oxford Road,
Manchester, M13 9PL, UK
and Room 400, 175 Fifth Avenue, New York, NY 10010, USA

Distributed exclusively in the USA and Canada
by St. Martin's Press, Inc., 175 Fifth Avenue, New York, NY 10010, USA

British Library cataloguing in publication data
  Wiener, Joel
  William Lovett. — (Lives of the left)
  1. Chartism. Lovett, William – Biographies
  I. Title   II. Series
  322.4'4'0924

Library of Congress cataloging in publication data
Wiener, Joel H.
  William Lovett / Joel Wiener.
     p.   cm. — (Lives of the left)
  Includes bibliographical references and index.
  ISBN 0-7190-2172-3: $40.00 (U.S.: est.).
  ISBN 0-7190-2173-1 (pbk.) : $15.00 (U.S. : est.)
  1. Lovett, William, 1800-1877. 2. Labor and laboring classes—Great
  Britain—Biography. 3. Chartism—Biography.
  I. Title   II. Series
  HD8393.L67W54 1989
  322'.2'0924—dc19

ISBN 0 7190 2172 3 *hardback*
ISBN 0 7190 2173 1 *paperback*

92
L911w

m.r

Set in Perpetua
by Koinonia Ltd, Manchester

Printed in Great Britain
by Hartnoll Ltd, Bodmin, Cornwall

Contents

Acknowledgements

I have incurred many obligations in writing this book and am more convinced than ever that scholarship is a collaborative endeavour. The staffs of various libraries were courteous and helpful to me. These included the British Library, the Birmingham Public Library, the Columbia University Library, the Public Record Office, and the New York Public Library. I am also grateful to the City College of the City University of New York for a paid sabbatical leave in the spring of 1987 which enabled me to complete the writing of this book.

I want particularly to thank the following friends and colleagues: Professor John Harrison, who shared with me a portion of his considerable knowledge about Lovett; Dr Brian Harrison for information about portraits of Lovett and his burial in Highgate Cemetery; Professor Gregory Claeys for help in reconstructing Lovett's involvement with the People's International League; Professor William Roberts for information about Lovett's relationship with Mazzini; Mrs Betty Bostetter for archival references and her general fund of knowledge. Dr Iorwerth Prothero and Dr David Howell read the manuscript carefully and saved me from factual errors as well as helping me to sharpen areas of interpretation. I am especially grateful to my wife Suzanne. Her unfailing patience, encouragement, and perceptive comments on the typescript are more appreciated than even she can know. Ernest and Ruth Poisson of Highgate have facilitated the research and writing of this book by the warmth of their hospitality on many occasions. I owe a considerable debt to them.

Introduction

William Lovett (1800-1877) is one of the most lauded working-class leaders of the early nineteen century. He has been praised effusively in terms of style and substance by many of the leading historians of the Labour movement. To G. D. H. Cole Lovett was an idealist, to Mark Hovell a leader of 'progressive' Chartism, to Max Beer an embodiment of 'intellectual and moral strength',[1] and to R. H. Tawney a 'Social Democrat' and the 'first and greatest of working-class educationalists'.[2] Among the older school of writers only Marxian historians like Theodore Rothstein have largely dissented from these judgments, on grounds of Lovett's ineffectualness and lack of revolutionary temperament rather than basic goals. Furthermore, Lovett has seemed to epitomise a capacious set of qualities, as pointed up in two recent essays whose conclusions, though favourable, are seemingly contradictory. The former Labour Party leader, Michael Foot, describes him as in 'the great tradition of our Labour movement'[3] while the more centrist Oxford historian Brian Harrison adjudges Lovett to be a part of the 'humane, participatory and libertarian tradition that the Victorians inherited from the eighteenth-century Enlightenment'.[4]

Lovett helped (and confused) his own cause immeasurably by publishing an autobiography, *Life and Struggles of William Lovett in Pursuit of Bread, Knowledge and Freedom*, in 1876, scarcely more than a year before his death. This classic account of working-class life portrays him as an artisan striving to overcome obstacles of poverty and educational disadvantage while pursuing economic and political justice. Lovett maintains that he was forced to do battle on two fronts: with the unreasoning and ill-bred left led by the Chartist leader, Feargus O'Connor, and with conservative Tories and Whigs on his right. His narrative is generally persuasive, although it is at times inconsistent and self-congratulatory. Indeed, Lovett's contributions to reform – especially his involvement with Chartism and its struggles for a democratic suffrage and the extension of adult education – are among the significant events of the Victorian years. He and his admirers make a compelling case for him as one of the inspiring leaders of the moderate working-class left in the nineteenth century.

Yet this picture requires modification. The problems in writing the biography of a working-class reformer are sometimes formidable because the documentation is often unequal to the task. This is in part true of Lovett, whose *Life and Struggles* overshadows all other sources. His participation in Chartism is fully described in the book, as well as in a number of printed and manuscript sources. But the earlier and later phases of his life are more difficult to reconstruct and even the Chartist years contain shadows and inconsistencies, a problem accentuated by Lovett's tendency to omit or 'reinterpret' in his autobiography material unfavourable to him. For example, historians who are predisposed to Lovett generally imprint a moderate interpretation on virtually all his actions. Yet as a presumed political rationalist and pioneer of education, he does not appear as consistently temperate on close analysis as he does from a distance. Lovett is capable of pettiness and bluster at times, and of a streak of political meanness. Sometimes his integrity dissolves into vindictiveness. There is also rhetorical violence in his language, at least until the early 1840s.

And as historians burrow ever more deeply into the interstices of nineteenth-century radicalism, they unravel complexities about working-class life that Tawney, Beer, Hovell and other admirers of Lovett were unaware of fifty years ago. For example, work by Dorothy Thompson, James Epstein, Iorwerth Prothero, and John Belchem makes clear the difficulty in categorising popular radicals as either 'moderate' or 'extreme', or in the case of Chartism, as exemplars of moral or physical force, the labels commonly affixed to the leaders of the movement. A fully-rounded portrait of Lovett must therefore be presented if his reputation as a leader of the moderate left is to be sustained in this first full biography of him. It must encompass warts as well as virtues, and take into account revisionist interpretations of Chartism and of nineteenth-century radicalism. Such a portrait, in the words of Thomas Carlyle, must resolve to tell 'all the truth so far as the biographer knows it'.

1 Early years

William Lovett was born in the small fishing village of Newlyn, Cornwall, on 8 May 1800. It is difficult to imagine a place more removed from the political and economic upheavals that sub-sequently defined the shape of his life and of the working-class struggle for reform. At the beginning of the nineteenth century, Newlyn had not yet become a magnet for the school of artists who were to make it famous. Nor did it count for much in economic terms. It abuts picturesque Mount's Bay, two miles farther than Penzance in the direction of Land's End, in the remote south-western corner of England. Modern tourism and industrial development have somewhat disfigured its charm, but at the time of Lovett's birth Newlyn was a sheltered hamlet dominated by the demands of the region's fishermen. Its lone road overlooked a busy harbour where pilchard and mackerel fishermen briskly plied their trade. Behind the harbour rows of thatched cottages ascended steeply to the hills beyond. In one of these cottages, near the site of a Methodist chapel which no longer exists, William Lovett was born and spent the early years of his life.

Lovett's father was the captain of a small boat, and died shortly before William was born; his mother, Kezia Green, sold fish in Penzance market. In economic terms Lovett's childhood was predictably difficult. He, a sister and three brothers were raised by his mother with the help of her relatives. The family's scanty income derived from the fishing trade, a precarious business even in its heyday. Lovett did not receive much in the way of a formal education nor the economic security vouchsafed to some other poor children of the region. He briefly attended dame schools in Newlyn and Penzance where he learned only the rudiments of mathematics and literacy. Yet, as he affirms in his *Life and Struggles* with a mixture of cantankerousness and admiration, respectability was at all times a family virtue. The young boy who stood almost paradigmatically for propriety and self-discipline in his later years was not permitted by his mother to mingle promiscuously with the other 'ignorant, idle and vicious boys'[1] who abounded in the streets of Penzance and Newlyn. Instead, like another working-class reformer of the period, Richard Carlile, who grew up in Ashburton, Devon, at nearly the same time, he was made to conform to a strict family upbringing.

Methodism was popular among Cornish fishermen and artisans in the early nineteenth century, and Lovett was subjected to its regimen of chapel-going and Sabbath observance. His reading, both at home and school, was primarily confined to religious literature. When, at the age of about eight, he contracted smallpox (a common disease in the West Country despite the recent introduction of vaccinations), his mother believed it to be an act of providence for the boy's rebelliousness. In his twenties, Lovett was to repudiate Methodism and become a deist and a 'practical' freethinker. Yet unlike Carlile and other freethinkers, he never entirely rejected the tenets of Christian belief. On the contrary, the morality and integrity which he may be seen to represent as a later spokesman for working-class radicalism remained broadly Christian at its core. Lovett's beliefs were to be based on a secularised version of Christian self-help. And although he championed religious freedom throughout his life (primarily meaning no compulsory sanctions against those dissenting from the Church of England), he reconciled himself somewhat to traditional Christianity in his later years.

Still, Lovett's somewhat austere childhood affected him in

obvious ways. For one thing it made him earnest, at times inflexibly so. Not even his most passionate admirers have attempted to imbue him with a sense of humour. Other reformers of the period occasionally veered into lightheartedness. Henry Hunt and Feargus O'Connor, for example, sometimes belittled their own pretensions even while engaged in raucous speechmaking; Henry Vincent, a Chartist orator who has been described as a 'cheerful puritan', specialised in mimicking his opponents. Lovett never expressed himself in either of these ways. He was as serious about reform as it is possible for a man to be. Utility was the wellspring of his conviction, determination its motive force. Above all, time was a precious commodity for Lovett. As he began to read controversial pamphlets and weighty tomes in his twenties, he eschewed frivolity, concentrating only upon things he regarded as worthwhile. A taut asceticism etched itself into his temperament, helping to give it shape, as it did for other working-class reformers of the period.

As absorbing and informative as the *Life and Stuggles* is, it lacks colour. There are only a few scenes of genuine passion in the book; instead, its author appears to be influenced from an early age by an abstract desire to gain political and social justice. Lovett reveals little about the texture of his boyhood. He recollects a few tales about 'goblins' and some of the eccentric characters whom he observed in his youth, especially during a brief period spent with a relative in Porthleven. Yet concerning these critically formative years of his life, there is little explanation of his passion for justice. One must search for clues and one set of experiences may be helpful. These involved press-gangs, of a kind still common in the ports and coastal villages of England in the early nineteeth century. Such gangs searched periodically for able-bodied seamen, especially during the final stages of the prolonged wars with France which finally came to an end in 1815. Lovett recollects the Cornish press-gangs being helped by soldiers with 'drawn cutlasses' who seized innocent victims and separated them from their families. In one instance (filtered through his memory thirty or so years later), a blind girl saved her father from such a gang, while 'half the women and boys of the neighborhood'[2] cheered lustily.

Yet although Lovett's sensibilities as a reformer were affected by this incident (and presumably by similar incidents which he does not record), it is clear that he was influenced primarily by the economic circumstances of his youth rather than by its political configuration. Poverty holds the key to an understanding of how a young craftsman from a Cornish fishing village was to become one of the leading urban radicals of his time. His dame school education was poor, though no worse than that received by most boys of his generation. Then, while in his early teens, he left school permanently and was apprenticed to several ropemakers in the Penzance area, beginning with an uncle. Ropemaking was a dying skill in Cornwall in the second decade of the nineteenth century as nautical ropes began to be replaced by chains, and Lovett's prospects were bad from the outset. He soon found ropemaking physically as well as economically insupportable.

For a time he tried fishing, though he failed at this too, because, as he tells us somewhat surprisingly, of an unaccustomed propensity to seasickness. He then began to work at carpentry, gradually honing his skills until he was good enough to secure a small income. This craft, as it turned out, was to be his trade for life. Yet for all practical purposes, Lovett was a displaced artisan from the outset, who was not directly affected by industrialisation but rather touched by many of the changes it introduced into Britain's economy, changes which made it increasingly difficult for skilled workers to compete with the products of machines. After several years of spasmodic work as a carpenter in Penzance and its surrounding neighbourhood, he decided to take the big plunge.

In June 1821, Lovett left the West Country for London, hoping to gain economic security and to advance his career prospects. Although he could not know it at the time, he was to spend nearly all of the remainder of his life in the nation's capital.

In London, Lovett translated his general skill at carpentry into cabinet-making, which comprised the various branches of the domestic furniture industry. For several years he attempted, with modest success, to find steady work as a cabinet-maker. On one occason he worked for a debtor in the Fleet Prison who then proceeded to dun him out of his wages. A saga of discouraging reversals is described in the *Life and Struggles*, as the young untutored Cornishman, speaking English self-consciously and with a broad regional dialect, tried to establish his claims in the metropolis. After a period of several years, Lovett achieved some success by obtaining regular employment in a shop near Tottenham Court Road. However he did not go through the required apprenticeship for cabinet-making, which created problems for him for a time. One time his fellow workers, resentful at his lack of training, set 'Mother Shorney' at him, meaning they attempted to drive him out of his shop by making life uncomfortable for him. He relates (somewhat unfashionably for a man who later became an advocate of temperance reform) that he won these workers over by standing them a round of drinks and pleading his case forthrightly. He was soon accepted into the London Society of Cabinet-Makers, the association which officially regulated conditions of work in the trade. Afterwards he was chosen president of the organisation, a position he held for several years. Thus at a time of economic transition in Britain, when customary restrictions were being loosened and a new industrial system was taking root, Lovett managed to gain a small measure of professional success.

During his initial years in London several eventful things happened in his life. In 1826 he married a young woman from Kent who was working as a lady's maid at the time. Mary Lovett was to be William's affectionate and loyal wife until his death in 1877, though the wedding was nearly cancelled when he unexpectedly refused to take the sacrament because of his newly-acquired belief in a Christianity without rituals or forms. Mary was an unobtrusive spouse with a conventional view of her role in life. She consoled her husband in difficult times and participated in some of his political activities. Accepting his belief that a wife should ideally be a philosophical companion to her spouse, she tried to read a great deal and to improve herself. They had two daughters, one of whom died in an accident as a child.

A second significant event in Lovett's early life in London was the beginning of his lengthy process of self-education, starting with membership of the London Mechanics' Institute and of a society of radical freethinkers known as the 'Liberals', who read and discussed books and tried to keep the flame of free discussion burning. For several years, beginning in the early 1820s, Lovett participated in weekly literary and philosophical debates sponsored by the Liberals. He made considerable use of their subscription library. There for the first time he read books as disparate and provocative as William Paley's *Evidences of Christianity* and Thomas Paine's *Age of Reason*, which won him over to a Christian deism. He attended lectures by radical orators like John Gale Jones, Richard Carlile, and Robert Taylor, the latter a well-known advocate of 'moral deism' based on astrological relationships. And as a member of the Liberals, Lovett essayed writing for newspapers on a variety of political and economic subjects; however, only a few were published in these years. By the mid-1820s, as he informs readers of his autobiography, he had become animated by a lifelong conviction as to the need to work for the 'happiness of the future'.

Historians including Eric Hobsbawm and Iorwerth Prothero have written insightfully about early nineteenth-century artisan

9

culture, and it is necessary to consider this general influence on Lovett's life. When, in the mid-1820s, he began for the first time to direct his attention to political and economic subjects, Britain was in the throes of its transformation from a pre-industrial society to one that was soon to be referred to as 'the workshop of the world'. Primarily in textile manufactures a factory system replaced clusters of small workshops, though more slowly than has been generally assumed. Industrial cities like Manchester and Leeds absorbed smaller towns and villages. The impact of economic change and urbanisation was experienced in miscellaneous ways. Craftsmen with developing political interests like Lovett, Carlile (tinworker), Henry Hetherington (printer), and Thomas Cooper (shoemaker) were entangled in this web of experience and forced to make adjustments to it.

Yet generalisations are difficult because the economic and cultural changes were more complicated than they appear. Lovett spent most of his life in London, not in the north of England where the more significant changes were taking place. He was not, therefore, either a direct observer of industrialisation or a victim of it; rather he was an involved bystander who found it impossible to extricate himself from many of its difficulties. In one sense, the version of working class radicalism that Lovett honed in the 1830s and 1840s and that became his major contribution to reform may be interpreted as a protest against industrialisation. More meaningfully, it represented an attempt by him and his followers to continue to live the kind of idealised pre-industrial life they had grown up with but which was, realistically, no longer possible.

Another caveat – partly contradicting the previous statement – is that, as the researches of John Breuilly and Raphael Samuel have shown, the line between artisans and semi-skilled and unskilled workers was not sharply drawn during this period. (Cabinet-making was itself a 'non-aristocratic' craft which was less highly regarded than other skilled occupations.) The economy did not advance seamlessly from one structure to another; changes were uneven and bumpy. In political terms, this meant that the 'moderate' ideas of Lovett were not always as different from those of northern leaders like Feargus O'Connor as has been assumed, notwithstanding the latter's use of a cruder rhetoric. Geographical and occupational variations were obviously crucial. But equally important was a feeling common to many poor people at the time that the authority both of the old state and the new industry were too oppressive. Thus the views of 'rational' reformers like Lovett and 'demagogic' ones like O'Connor (the adjectives progressive and reactionary are sometimes used in a similar way) have much in common, as will be seen later.

Still there *was* a distinctive artisanal culture, and this helped to frame Lovett's life, however blurred it may have become in the turbulent world of radical politics. Craftsmen like Lovett who contended manfully for survival and achieved their limited successes with their own hands came to believe in the virtues of self-help and independence. They were eager to improve themselves intellectually as well as financially. They embodied egalitarian attitudes which were rooted in individualism. They believed in political democracy. And organisations like the Liberals, which circulated books and sponsored lectures and debates on self-improving issues, gained support from them, particularly in the coffeehouses of Clerkenwell and the West End.

Lovett regularly attended meetings of the Liberals and other organisations throughout the 1820s, absorbing their credo of political and economic regeneration. He studied grammatical texts and avariciously devoured books on politics, philosophy, and religion, many of which advocated unorthodox opinions. Like thousands of other intellectually budding artisans, he nurtured an inordinate faith in education. It was during these years when he worked hard as a cabinet-maker and also for a brief

11

naged a pastry and confectionary shop with his wife,
.......he blazed the path of autodidacticism so exuberantly
described in the pages of the *Life and Struggles*. He tells its readers
that, in the 1820s, 'My mind seemed to be awakened to a new
mental existence; new feelings, hopes, and aspirations sprang up
within me'.[3] Education was the foundation of his belief in
improvement because economic security and political change
developed from it. It was the means to a rational life; without
it, the privileges of favoured groups would continue to be an
insuperable obstacle to the majority of workingmen; with it,
these would be overcome. Thus, craftsmen like Lovett sought
to elevate their status. In political terms their chief goal was
autonomy: in Lovett's words, to 'stand erect, conscious of our
own worth, power and importance in society'.[4]

Working-class assertiveness sometimes took the form of
imitating the social aspirations of their 'betters'. It is misleading,
however, to think of most of these reforming artisans as class–collaborationist, or labour–aristocratic in the sense in which Marxian
historians use the term. If Lovett's contribution to popular
radicalism is to be properly understood, the words in the subtitle
of his autobiography – 'Bread, Knowledge, Freedom' – must be
taken seriously. At the base of his personal superstructure lay
his experience as a working craftsman, dependent on manual
skills and psychological satisfactions; at the apex was his determination to achieve fundamental change. Somewhere in between
Lovett grappled, at times fitfully and inconsistently, with the
entrenched privileges which he believed had to be rooted out.

The thread holding these miscellaneous ideas together for him
in the 1820s was economic co-operation, which, as J. F. C.
Harrison and other historians have shown, permeated many
aspects of working-class culture. The 'economy of co-operation'
embodied the writings of diverse thinkers like William
Thompson, George Mudie, John Gray, Abram Combe and Robert

Owen, who specifically advocated schemes for building villages
of co-operation and ideal communities like that commenced in
New Harmony, Indiana, in 1825. Owen wanted to use these
communities as a springboard to replace the competitive
economic system which, he believed, was diminishing the possibilities for human happiness. In the words of Mudie, the editor
of the *Economist*, an Owenite magazine, such communities 'offered
the only means of giving abundance, and intellectual and moral
excellence to all mankind'.[5]

For several years, beginning in the mid-1820s, Lovett supported such communites. He was enthusiastic about the need to
apply human effort 'for the benefit of all in common, to the
lightening of their toil and the increase of their comforts. . .'.[6]
He favoured small co-operative villages to be established with
the capital of workingmen, in preference to the somewhat larger
communities envisaged by Owen which were to be externally
funded. The communities advocated by Lovett were self-govern-
ing, with their structure and rules to be determined by majority
vote. Then poverty, crime and other social evils would disappear,
to be replaced by an educated population with unlimited access
to the physical and intellectual comforts of life. As Lovett told
those present at an Owenite meeting in 1830: 'The life, labour,
and property of every man should be secured to him; and. . .
each should be responsible to all if he violated that constitution'.[7]

Yet artisans like Lovett, along with many domestic and factory
workers, were also attracted to the ideal of co-operation for
reasons other than its link with communitarianism. Many reformers perceived in the philosophy of economic co-operation
a generalised commitment to social equality, without necessarily
implying an end to private ownership of property. Others played
down the anti-individualism characteristic of co-operation (and
specifically of Owenism) in favour of moral freedom and an
absence of economic restraints. Lovett was inconsistent and

ambivalent in his thinking. He and other radical reformers attacked the competitive system while using co-operative ideas primarily as a way of translating their desire for economic autonomy into political terms. In their minds they merged economic and political reform, a position anathema to Owenites, who favoured only the former.

Economic co-operation therefore gave Lovett and his associates in the Liberals and other organisations a foundation upon which to attack the wealth and power of ruling groups. To be a co-operator in the 1820s, one did not necessarily have to reject private property. Lovett wavered for several years on this critical point as he attempted fitfully to locate his position along the trajectory of reform. Until about 1832, he advocated both economic co-operation and political reform. Most of his writings and speeches on the subject of co-operation were phrased in suitably abstract terms. Yet he could be harsh and militant on the subject of property, a fact sometimes conveniently overlooked by his moderate admirers. Thus, at a meeting of co-operators in April 1830, he moved a resolution calling for the forcible equalisation of labour and goods. On another occasion in the same year he attacked non-producers. They were, he asserted, 'monsters', who must be eliminated because they 'prey upon the vitals of society'.[8]

As well as providing him with the skeleton of a political philosophy, co-operation gave Lovett his first institutional base in radical politics. Beginning in the early 1820s various Owenite associations came into existence whose purpose was to disseminate co-operative doctrines among the working classes. The most important of these groups was the London Co-operative Society, founded in 1824 in part to restore 'the whole produce of labour to the labourer'. In 1827 the London Co-operative Society established the First London Co-operative Trading Association with premises in Greville Street, Clerkenwell. Shortly afterwards

Lovett was appointed to the position of shopkeeper to the latter association. This group ('a mere trading association', in Owen's contemptuous view) bought goods from weavers, artisans and other workingmen and sold them cheaply to its members. By eliminating middlemen and 'non-producers' from the economic system it intended to pave the way for a restructuring which would place trade and industry under the control of labour. Although such a restructuring never took place the group was in effect a forerunner of the Rochdale Co-operative Association of 1844. Lovett resigned as shopkeeper after several months when his salary was reduced due to substantial losses by the society. But he remained an active member for several years.

During this time of increased political activity, Lovett continued to espouse economic co-operation vigorously in speeches and occasional essays written for working-class newspapers. Producers must be justly rewarded, he affirmed on many occasions, while workingmen were entitled to the full value of their contribution. These ideas derived particularly from lectures by Thomas Hodgskin at the London Mechanics' Institute in the 1820s, which Lovett attended, and from Hodgskin's popular tract, *Labour Defended Against the Claims of Capital, or the Unproductiveness of Capital Proved*, published in 1825. Hodgskin advocated economic individualism but Lovett interpreted his labour theory of value in terms of his reading of Owenism. The purpose of society, according to Lovett, was to equalise 'natural disproportions' and eliminate selfishness. 'Equal rights and equal happiness' would follow inevitably from such changes, beginning at the level of wholesale trading. Competition, which generated extremes of wealth and misery, would go the way of other extinct forms of life once reason was allowed to exercise its untrammeled influence. Increasingly Lovett began to emphasise his belief in the importance of private property. Yet he tempered this with an ardent commitment to the 'social principle' of a shared activity,

15

in which men would work 'with, instead of against, each other. . . rendering. . . productive powers of general utility, and for cultivation of the social virtues. . .'.[9]

Up to about 1832, Lovett was a leading exponent of economic co-operation, and his political beliefs and activism took shape from the context of this commitment. During these years of a revived working-class movement for parliamentary reform after the lull of the early and mid-1820s, a number of radical reformers became prominent. For example, William Cobbett and Richard Carlile effectively mined the techniques of popular journalism, while Henry Hunt excelled as a public speaker. Lovett lacked outstanding ability in both areas. He was a quiet, tenacious man who preferred to master the intricacies of secretarial work. In competition with reformers who vied for the public spotlight, he invariably opted for a low-key approach. He mastered details and became adept at managing small committees. Within a few years he found his niche as an organiser of procedure, and in this unlikely guise he emerged as a successful leader of reform.

As the paid part-time secretary of the British Association for the Promotion of Co-operative Knowledge (BAPCK) from January until the autumn of 1831 (this major organisation of economic co-operators was founded in May 1829 by a group of London workingmen), Lovett's chief task was to maintain links with many local Owenite societies affiliated to it. He co-ordinated the financial and other activities of more than 200 corresponding organisations. He managed the bazaar of the BAPCK where substantial quantities of goods were exchanged. At quarterly meetings of the organisation, its members ratified policy decisions taken by the executive committee, on which Lovett sat. He performed a visible role at these meetings. He was a chief defender of the BAPCK's policies and was instrumental in defining its political and economic goals. In his speeches, as reported in the *Weekly Free Press*, he urged two objectives upon the organisation:

to propagate the ideal of economic co-operation and to try to bring about a series of political reforms, including an extension of the franchise, education for the poor, and an untaxed press. The focus on political goals generated disagreement within the organisation, and Owen condemned the BAPCK for diverting its energies into parliamentary agitation and adopting a 'storekeeping' view of public issues.

In April 1832, Lovett played an active role at the Third Co-operative Congress, held in London, which he helped to organise. He spoke with considerable bitterness about the scenes of wretchedness he had witnessed among the Spitalfields weavers, 'the demon of famine wasting their vitals, while they industriously toil at their looms for sixteen hours daily, without being able to earn sufficient to satisfy the cravings of hunger. . .'.[10] He backed a proposal at the Congress to establish an 'Incipient Community' based upon the subscriptions of those who actually joined, an idea opposed by Owen, who favoured a more comprehensive approach to community-building. This incident caused Lovett to distance himself from Owen and in his autobiography he is critical of the latter's 'vain-glorious' temperament. Still, he remained sympathetic to Owen's general views. In 1834, he supported the Grand National Consolidated Trades Union, an attempt by Owen and some of his followers to make use of the burgeoning trade union movement for co-operative purposes. However, by the early 1830s political and educational goals began to absorb an increasing amount of his time and energy. It is to these we must now turn.

2 The forging of a radical

In his *Life and Struggles* Lovett devotes only thirty-eight pages to his involvement in the political battles of the early 1830s, that is, prior to the establishment of the Working Men's Association in June 1836. Nonetheless, these are crucial years in the history of working-class radicalism. They witnessed epochal struggles for parliamentary reform and an unstamped press, the effort to establish a national trade union movement, and the emergence of related issues, including opposition to the New Poor Law Act of 1834 and agitation for factory legislation. Lovett was at the centre of several of these events. He was influenced by them. In part he achieved prominence as a participant in them. And his contribution to radical reform, though less visible in the early 1830s than during the subsequent Chartist years, was almost as notable. Yet he chooses to de-emphasise this period in his autobiography, converting it into a relatively minor episode in a long, eventful political career. Many historians have, perhaps unwittingly, followed his lead.

Why the distortion? Undoubtedly, the chief reason has to do with the structure of his political life as he and his enthusiasts have chosen to interpret it. Lovett the rationalistic author of the *Life and Struggles* depicts himself as a steadfast opponent of extremists on both the left and right. He is the quintessential man of moderation who inevitably sets himself against lawbreaking. Thus he retrospectively observes that if 'the violence and folly of the hot-brained few (could) have been restrained (in the early 1830s) . . . a far larger amount of good might have been effected'.[1] Chartism would have gained its ends by indirection; while some of the leading reform movements of the decade, which predated it and acted as a stimulus to the larger agitation, would have been satisfactorily concluded. There is some validity to Lovett's reading of events. It may well be that less rhetorical violence and more collaboration among reformers would have yielded better results. But consistency *after the fact* is always easy to secure, as Lovett's own career demonstrates.

Coming to political maturity at a time of deeply-felt grievances, he was not as frequently a critic of the 'hot-brained few' and their 'violence and folly' as he would like others to believe. Like his fellow radicals, he was passionate about the issues of the day and always identified with the poor. He wrote and spoke fervidly, expounding a traditional corpus of radical ideas, while occasionally saying and doing things he regretted. This need not necessarily be a source of embarrassment to him, though it meant he had implicitly to repudiate some of his earlier positions. The pressures of outside events, fluctuating friendships, and organisational entanglements imposed inconsistencies upon Lovett and his fellow agitators. Class loyalties were hammered out on the anvil of fundamental political and economic antagonisms. In such circumstances, it is not surprising that unpredictable things happened. At the least, expediency sometimes overrode principle. Lovett's commitments were still relatively unformed, and not until the early 1840s did he emerge consistently and unambiguously as a proponent of moderate reform.

In the late 1820s, Lovett began to make a series of significant political friendships. He got to know Henry Hunt and William Cobbett. He became acquainted with John Gast, the secretary of the shipwrights' union, and participated in the Benefit Societies campaign of 1828-29, which led to the passage of friendly society legislation favourable to the working classes. Most important, he began to work closely with Henry Hetherington, James Watson and John Cleave, three working-class reformers whose fortunes were to be linked intimately with his own for many years. Hetherington, Watson and Cleave were participants in the co-operative movement and members of the BAPCK. Along with Lovett, their interests were becoming focused on politics. Increasingly they were coming to believe that political power had first to be won: then the requisite social and economic changes would follow, including a reconstitution of property relationships. In July 1829, the four reformers helped to found the Radical Reform Association, an organisation composed chiefly of artisans, which championed universal manhood suffrage during the seventeen months of its existence.

The RRA has been inexplicably overlooked by historians of radicalism. It deserves rehabilitation. For one thing, it was the first London-based working-class organisation of the period to champion consistently a democratic suffrage. As such, it criticised at times even the programme of its mentor, Hunt, who was elected to Parliament from Preston in December 1830, and during the next two years was to be the most vocal (if occasionally inconsistent) opponent of the Whig measure of parliamentary reform from the radical left. The RRA also pursued a policy of non-co-operation with middle-class reformers in London, who began to organise at the outset of 1830 to gain a limited measure of parliamentary reform.

From a reading of newspaper accounts and information sent to the Home Office by informers (who were often unreliable), it is clear that Lovett was actively involved with the RRA, though not notably on the side of the 'moderates'. He rejected petitioning as a device to redress grievances and refused to compromise the political rights of the working classes, which meant he would accept nothing less than universal manhood suffrage, a demand of many radical reformers from the days of Thomas Hardy's London Corresponding Society of the 1790s. And Lovett repeatedly made clear his belief in the need for economic justice for the poor. He participated in meetings held by the RRA at the Rotunda, a building on the south side of the Thames, where he and his associates (including the freethinker Julian Hibbert) gained a reputation for being extremists. At one Rotunda meeting Lovett performed a public act which, not surprisingly, he does not mention in his *Life and Struggles*. He moved successfully that copies of *The Times* and the *Weekly Dispatch*, two papers deemed hostile to the interests of the working classes, be burnt. The resolution was carried out by those present at the meeting, including Lovett.

The organisational history of radical reform in London in the years 1829 to 1832 is complex. It reflects primarily the shifting currents of the parliamentary reform campaign. Between the introduction of the first bill for the extension of the suffrage in the House of Commons by Lord John Russell in March 1831, and final passage of the Reform Act in June 1832, a series of events supervened. These included an agitation for universal suffrage organised by Lovett and other radical reformers; a threatened run on the banks initiated by 'moderate' reformers with ties to Whig and Radical Members of Parliament such as Francis Place; riots in Bristol, Nottingham, Derby, and elsewhere directed against opponents of reform; and the formation by reformers of political unions throughout the country to carry on the struggle for an extension of the franchise.

During the years 1830-32 working-class and middle-class reformers gave voice to their respective blueprints for reform, that is household suffrage and universal suffrage. At times, they combated one another; at other times, they worked together spasmodically to increase pressure on the Whig government of Earl Grey, which vacillated in its support for reform. Some newly-established unions dissolved rapidly from lack of support; others gained strength from the escalating series of events. One radical idea – for example, that assessed taxes not be paid until reform was won, or, at Lovett's suggestion, that working-class lodgers withhold the payment of rent – gave way to another. Oratorical sparks set off verbal conflagrations in the coffeehouses and taverns of London where artisans gathered, as feelings became intensified and informers did their best to exacerbate an already tense situation.

Lovett was an enthusiastic participant in these events. He attended numerous meetings and wrote articles for radical newspapers, including a few verses. Simultaneously, he continued to work as a cabinet-maker and to limit his political activities to evenings and weekends. In March 1830, he and several associates (including Hunt) helped to establish the Metropolitan Political Union, a short-lived organisation whose aims differed from that of the RRAJ. It was basically a middle-class-dominated association which received support from radical Members of Parliament like Daniel O'Connell and Joseph Hume, and from the energetic Francis Place who began at about this time to refer scornfully to Lovett and his friends as 'Rotundanists'. Unlike the RRA, the MPU espoused an 'Effectual and Radical Reform in the Commons House of Parliament', a formulation which favoured household rather than universal suffrage. The MPU urged an alliance between middle-class and working-class reformers, encouraging both groups to strive for gains by 'just, legal, constitutional and peaceful means'. Given the differences of emphasis between the RRA and the more conservative MPU, it is easy to understand why an excitable young reformer like Lovett, with a developing sense of grievance about his own condition and that of the nation at large, would have felt more comfortable with the former.

Lovett was one of the thirty-six original members of the council of the MPU. But he and Hetherington resigned in the summer of 1830 to protest against the organisation's failure to endorse universal suffrage and to support wholeheartedly the July revolution in France, which overthrew the Bourbon monarchy. Several of Lovett's associates, including Watson and William Carpenter, remained active in both the MPU and the RRA, and by so doing, declared their belief in class collaboration. But Lovett was attracted to the RRA, which aggressively championed the cause of the working classes. It was the first of several occasions in his life when he opposed the suggestion of an alliance between middle-class and working-class reformers.

In September 1831 Lovett became a member of still another political organisation, the National Union of the Working Classes, a successor (via the short-lived Metropolitan Trades Union) to the RRA, which was dissolved at the end of 1830, and the BAPCK, whose demise occurred in the autumn of 1831. The NUWC fused the twin demands of economic co-operation and political democracy, in line with its objective of working-class 'justice in legislation . . . and (their) rights and liberties'.[2] Lovett was a key member of the organisation who contributed to many of its activites up to the summer of 1832. It is not a period of his life that has received enough attention, though given the unfair 'extremist' label applied to the NUWC by Place and others, that is perhaps understandable.

The NUWC was a ginger group which helped to build support for radical political reform and universal suffrage. Like the RRA, it met regularly at the Rotunda, regarded as a hotbed of sedition by opponents of reform and the informers who frequented its premises. (Place and other proponents of household suffrage depicted the 'Rotundanists' as dangerous revolutionaries and in the Home Office files there is a reference to Lovett as a 'Rotunda Radical'.) Yet the NUWC strongly promoted the virtues of political education. It formed study classes along Methodist lines; organised weekly meetings where contentious public issues were debated; gave support to the *Poor Man's Guardian*, the foremost radical penny periodical of the day; and influenced the lives of several thousand politically conscious workingmen in London. Operating within the ideological contours of the 'old radicalism', with its rhetorical assaults upon the corrupt trinity of kings, lords and priests, the NUWC contributed to the development of working-class consciousness, though in a pre-capitalist sense.

Beginning in November 1831, Lovett held a seat on the general committee of the NUWC, which framed resolutions for the organisation's weekly meetings. He was also one of twenty-four class leaders who met regularly with small groups of workingmen to discuss political and economic texts. And he and James Watson wrote the rules for the organisation, including a widely-circulated section grandiloquently titled the 'Declaration of the National Union of the Working Classes'.

The Declaration is a signpost to Lovett's thinking in the early 1830s. Like its American and French models, it contains a brief general statement expounding the philosophy of the organisation followed by specific proposals for reform. The leading influence was Thomas Paine. Lovett and Watson incorporated into the Declaration allusions to the *Rights of Man*, a seminal text among radical artisans at the time. They presented a case for natural rights, which was posited as the foundation of working-class freedom. The Declaration proposes that distinctions of birth based on heredity be abolished and that every adult male be guaranteed 'a free voice in determining the nature of the laws. . .'.[3]

Having affirmed the importance of a democratic political structure, the Declaration alludes to other reforms, including freedom of the press, full legal equality, and universal education. With the help of Paine, Lovett and Watson made the point that 'hereditary distinctions of birth' have unjustly robbed the people of the common benefits of the earth. Their objective, however, was not to interfere with private property which, if 'honestly acquired', is 'inviolable'; rather, they wanted to obtain the full proceeds of labour for every workingman. The ultimate sanction presented was the abstract one: that is, the obligation to resist government should it ignore its duties and fail to institute laws for the '*common benefit* in the protection and security of all the people'.

Notwithstanding his joint authorship of the Declaration, it is less by the articulation of theory that Lovett's political and social convictions at this time of crisis can be gauged than by tangible actions. In speeches delivered at NUWC meetings at the Rotunda (which were reprinted in the *Poor Man's Guardian* and other unstamped penny papers), he vigorously attacked the 'want and distress' afflicting the poor in London's East End, particularly the silk weavers of Spitalfields. Lovett's continuing efforts to gain security for his family intensified his commitment to economic justice. At one general meeting of the NUWC, he proclaimed a willingness to lead the fight for bread even if this meant taking up arms. Lovett put two questions to his audience: 'whether vast possessions enjoyed by the aristocracy should remain in their hands'; and whether 'fundholders' and 'placemen' should continue to profit from their oppression. The answers were self-evident to him. 'Public plunderers and private speculators' must be compelled to make amends for their misdeeds. Only when this happened, he told Place in a subsequent letter, might it be said that workingmen had 'planted the seeds of regeneration, the fruits of which will be reaped by posterity'.[5] As if to give support to this position, Lovett, John Cleave and Thomas Wakley, the crusading editor of the *Lancet*, conducted an investigation for the NUWC into conditions at a workhouse in Spitalfields. They discovered 'unpaved yards, and filthy courts, and the want of drainage and cleansing, (which) rendered [the silkweavers'] houses hotbeds of disease. . .'.[6]

As a leading member of the NUWC, Lovett once again opposed efforts to secure an alliance between working-class and middle-class reformers. This time his intervention was crucial. In October

1831, Place and other reformers established the National Political Union as a successor organisation to the Metropolitan Political Union. The NPU was created at the time of the Bristol riots when agitation on the subject of parliamentary reform was nearing its culmination. The purpose of the new organisation (like that of the Birmingham Political Union, founded in January 1830 by Thomas Attwood and other moderate reformers) was to effectuate a class alliance: 'not a Union of the Working Classes, nor of the Middle Classes, nor of any other Class, but of all Reformers, of the masses and of the millions'.[7] In part this meant winning over the support of the 'Rotundanists' for more limited goals than universal suffrage.

Lovett was considered by Place to be a particularly influential participant in the NUWC, and with the latter's support he was appointed to the provisional council of the NPU for three months. From the outset, however, his feelings and those of Cleave, his closest ally at the time, were made clear. Both men maintained that, as a litmus test of goodwill towards the working classes, the NPU must publicly endorse universal suffrage and the election of annual parliaments. Nothing less than this was acceptable. At a tense public meeting held at the Crown and Anchor tavern in the Strand, with Sir Francis Burdett and other prominent reformers present, Lovett rejected any compromise of principle. He asserted that 'there was no use in preaching up patience to the starving people of this country – to talk to them of patience and policy was only mocking their sufferings'.[8] His views were unacceptable to most of those present, who, according to the report in the *Poor Man's Guardian*, interrupted Lovett with 'hisses and loud cries of "off".' The result was a defeat for Cleave and Lovett, and an end to the possibility of an alliance across class lines.

Lovett did not leave the NPU immediately. He served on its council for the full three months and participated in several more meetings. At the same time, he gave increasing attention to the activities of the NUWC. In December 1831, when the first formal elections to the council for the NPU were held, he was not chosen as a working-class delegate although his name was on the original slate of candidates. Subsequently he ceased to have anything to do with the organisation. The NPU continued to pursue its campaign for parliamentary reform along the lines of the £10 household franchise which was adopted into law in June 1832, while many members of the NUWC, including Lovett, strongly opposed this measure in the belief that it did not go nearly far enough to meet the demands of the poor, who continued to be denied the vote. This second failed attempt at class collaboration, with Lovett taking a visible position in opposition, is notable in view of his subsequent attempts to unite moderate Chartists with middle-class Anti-Corn Law reformers.

Two events during 1831-32 further document Lovett's attitudes towards reform. The first, which thoroughly radicalised him, involved his refusal to serve in the militia. Although G. D. H. Cole's statement that this incident made Lovett a 'national political figure' is somewhat exaggerated, it was nonetheless important. In January 1831, Lovett inserted a paragraph in one of William Carpenter's unstamped *Political Letters and Pamphlets*, suggesting that people 'fill up' their militia papers: that is, declare themselves exempt from their required service on the ground that they had 'neither *voice* nor *vote* in the making of the laws . . . (and) no property but . . . *labour*, which is not protected'.[9] Such a challenge was noteworthy because in the absence of a standing army the local militia performed many military and law enforcement duties, and it was the practice to draw names periodically for service.

In April, after Lovett's 'no-vote no-militia' plan was formally endorsed by the NUWC, his name was drawn for service. Almost certainly, this was in retaliation for his outspokenness. As anticipated, he refused to serve when actually called before the Deputy

Lieutenant of Middlesex County in September, or to accept the alternative of paying for a substitute. He took an unyielding position, alleging that 'poor and weak as I am, I resist . . . the power of might, the power of despotism'.[10] To accept militia service would, Lovett affirmed, compel him 'to be a cruel instrument in the hands of the oppressors'.[11] The ensuing controversy became a *cause célèbre* in London's working-class circles and considerably enhanced Lovett's reputation for integrity and courage.

Although his associates in the NUWC sought to obstruct the legal process, Lovett was fined £15 for his refusal. His personal property, including most of his household furniture, was sold at auction. Hetherington and other reformers condemned this 'undisguised, downright, absolute robbery',[12] and collected subscriptions to aid Lovett. In the House of Commons, Joseph Hume initiated a debate on the subject. He argued that militia service was a tax on the urban poor because most of those called were unable to fulfil their duty and elected to pay substitutes instead. Nothing immediately developed from this opposition. On the other hand, Lovett became embittered by his treatment. As a result of the actions taken against him, he was forced into a desperate economic struggle for several years which strengthened his identification with the poor. Writing in 1837 with the militia incident in mind, he described the world cynically and defiantly as a 'hell of toil, of poverty, and crime'.

The other event of these years, imposed on Lovett rather than 'created' by him, had the paradoxical effect of making him more moderate. In February 1832, the Grey government proclaimed a 'public day of fasting and humiliation' whose purpose was to encourage people to pray for an end to the cholera, which was taking a heavy toll in the nation's cities. Radical reformers considered this a profanation at a time when many people lacked sufficient food. The NUWC dubbed it a 'Farce Day'. In the words of Hetherington's *Poor Man's Guardian*, it was 'a dangerous mockery – more calculated to excite than appease the anger of an omniscient Almighty'.[13] Lovett and his colleagues decided to celebrate the 'Farce Day' in their own fashion. They made arrangements to distribute food to groups of unemployed and hungry people. At the same time, they initiated preparations for a series of banquets in the evening, to be accompanied by the singing of patriotic songs and speeches attacking the hypocrisy of the government and calling for reforms. Small bands were to provide appropriate music for the occasion.

On 21 March, the appointed day, thousands of reformers set off from Finsbury Square in north London, intending to walk peaceably to Westminster as a means of displaying their strength. What happened next is not precisely clear. But policemen, who were out in force, rapidly dispersed the marchers into small groups. An altercation took place near Tottenham Court Road, which did *not* involve Lovett but led to several arrests. However Lovett, James Watson, and William Benbow, a more militant reformer, were arrested by the police and accused of encouraging a mob to throw stones and destroy property.

The trial of the three men was held in May at the Middlesex Sessions. Amid popular acclamation, they were acquitted of charges of unlawful assembly and intending to cause a breach of the peace. But it is Lovett's reaction to this incident which offers a pointer to his evolution as a radical leader. At his trial, he expressed bitterness towards those who had arrested him and confined him to a damp prison cell for eight hours before he was freed on bail. He put several loaded questions to the jurors: 'How much longer are we to wait with patience, before we are allowed to enjoy the fruits of our own industry? How much longer do they expect us to wait before we throw off the incubus that presses us down to the earth?'[14] In Lovett's opinion, the law was a mockery; it was obscurely worded and unjust, and he had been threatened with punishment while behaving throughout the day in a 'peaceable and orderly' fashion.

Yet, his anger with Benbow was greater. Benbow, Lovett believed, had actually engaged in violent acts, which were unacceptable. During these formative years as he developed ideas about the substance and tactics of reform, Lovett was often self-contradictory. He was not a 'moderate', at least with any consistency. But he was generally opposed to violence. Sometimes, in an abstract statement like the Declaration of the NUWC, he implied that physical force was acceptable. Yet, in most instances he came down on the side of non-violence, though without necessarily accepting the necessity to obey unjust laws. On the other hand, he believed Benbow to be a different breed: a man who was ready to use force to achieve specific political goals. As a result, shortly after the trial, Lovett denounced Benbow for his violent behaviour on the 'Farce Day' and for several years after the two men engaged in a bitter feud. Amid a welter of accusations and counter-charges, Lovett withdrew from the council of the NUWC, while retaining membership in the organisation. In the following months, he spoke occasionally at NUWC meetings but for all intents and purposes his involvement with the organisation was at an end. Thus this incident, which improved Lovett's standing in radical circles, strengthened his later claims to have been an advocate of moral reform all along.

The one outstanding political agitation that Lovett was involved with in the early 1830s was the 'war of the unstamped'. Between 1830 and 1836 working-class and middle-class reformers pressed hard for the removal of the stamp duty on newspapers (imposed in 1712) and several other 'taxes on knowledge', including those on advertisements and paper. They maintained that the 4d newspaper tax in particular prevented cheap periodicals and newspapers from circulating. Workingmen were, therefore, deprived of the means of gaining political knowledge. In the words of Cleave, a leader of the campaign against the duty:

'The people were determined to be represented in the press as well as in the legislature, and to be no longer contented with a system which applied learning and intelligence to the worst of purposes, making the poor poorer, and the rich more rich'.[15]

Opposition to the taxes on knowledge took several forms, including the drafting of petitions to Parliament and, more effectively, the publication and sale of several hundred unstamped periodicals. This illegal method of defiance involved the distribution of papers through a political network controlled by the NUWC and other working-class associations. Lovett was not intimately connected with the journalism of the campaign as were his colleagues Watson, Cleave, and Hetherington. He wrote occasionally for the *Poor Man's Guardian*, the *Destructive*, and other penny papers, and helped to distribute them. But he did not publish or edit any journals. Instead he performed a quietly effective administrative role in the campaign, which he later characterised as 'one of the most important political movements that I was ever associated with'.[16] He held the positions of sub-treasurer and secretary of a 'Victim Fund', established in July 1831 to provide financial aid to the hundreds of vendors and publishers who were arrested and incarcerated for violating the stamp laws. Lovett contributed 1s weekly to the fund from his own small income (a major expenditure for him) and helped to make the fund an effective part of the campaign. Although it distributed less than £400 overall, the fund facilitated the enlistment of substitute publishers and vendors, which made it difficult for the authorities to eviscerate the 'human wave' of volunteers confronting them.

Lovett also participated in other ways in the 'war of the unstamped'. When Hetherington, who published the *Poor Man's Guardian*, was seeking to evade the tentacles of the Stamp Office in 1834, he transferred ownership of his printing presses to his friend, who kept them for him so as to prevent their confiscation.

Lovett also covertly assisted with the distribution of the illegal papers to booksellers and vendors in London and the provinces. He made speeches denouncing the taxes and supporting those who undertook risks in defiance of the law. And in the final two years of the agitation, as the government headed by Lord Melbourne came under increasing pressure to make concessions, Lovett again employed his clerical skills to good effect.

In 1834, he became secretary of a committee established for the purpose of paying off the fines of Hetherington and Cleave, who had been arrested shortly before. Two years later, just before the Whigs agreed reluctantly to reduce the tax to 1*d* (while tightening enforcement of the law), Lovett was appointed secretary to still another committee, known as the 'Association of Working Men to Procure a Cheap and Honest Press'. This organisation was funded by Dr John Black, a reformer who had come to London by way of Kentucky. Its objective was to eliminate the remaining penny duty. In the Address of the Association, which Lovett wrote, he attacked the 'bitterest oppression' of the remaining penny and once more put the central question that he and other poor reformers had been asking for several years: whether it was 'just to mark out our class for so cruel an exclusion from the countless benefits and peculiarly inestimable gratification of possessing newspapers?'[17] The Association existed for several months before giving way to its much better-known successor, the Working Men's Association, which Lovett founded in June 1836.

The battle for an untaxed press had a significant impact on Lovett's career. As two accounts of this crucial episode in the history of radicalism have shown, it was an issue that moved reformers in different directions. On the one hand, it encouraged a belief in non-violent means of agitation. Lovett and other reformers canonised newspapers precisely because, in his words, they prefigured 'THE COMING AGE OF FREEDOM, PEACE

AND BROTHERHOOD'. If arguments for change could be rationally deployed in a setting of unrestrained give and take, conditions would almost certainly improve. This political conviction became a tenet of faith during the course of the six-year struggle in which freedom to express ideas was a central call to battle along with the right to educate.

Lovett's self-improving activities and participation in discussion groups like the Liberals on a regular basis since the 1820s had pointed the way to this conviction. 'Mental and moral improvement' were a desideratum for him because they held the key to advancement. Thus in 1833, midway through the repeal campaign, Lovett opened a coffee shop and reading room in Greville Street, on the very site of the defunct Owenite ventures he had participated in. For more than three years, with the help of his wife and sister, he struggled to make the reading room a success. On Saturday evenings recitations for 'mutual improvement' took place, and on Sundays, when poor workingmen were supposed to be in church, Lovett and his friends discussed books and engaged in conversations about political and religious subjects. These educational activities deeply affected his future outlook and they anticipated his identification with moral force Chartism.

Yet there was another side to the 'war of the unstamped', which must also be taken into account in assessing Lovett's development. The battle with the government strengthened class feelings among poor reformers. Lovett condemned obstructions to press freedom not only for obvious educational reasons but because, in his view, they kept printed matter in the control of 'monied men' and their aristocratic and clerical patrons. Thus for him and others the battle for a free press acquired class connotations. Poor workingmen read and distributed illegal penny papers because they believed the laws unjustly discriminated against them. As in Lovett's 'no-vote no-musket' campaign, those needing the press most were believed to be deprived of it by virtue of their poverty and powerlessness. Thus Lovett and hundreds of other activists showed their willingness to defy laws which they considered unjust. Illegality was for him an acceptable means in the circumstances (the only effective means) to rectify an evil situation. This militant side of the repeal movement intensified Lovett's emotional ties to his fellow workingmen. It allows us a glimpse of the 'other' Lovett, more committed and angry, who does not emerge as clearly from the many favourable accounts written about him.

Lovett's distrust of, even hatred for, the middle classes during these years is obvious, although he worked closely with them from time to time in the unstamped campaign. He believed it was important for poor people to secure the 'fruits of victory' on their own because, as he told readers of one unstamped newspaper, the middle classes 'having once effected their object . . . will turn around and bully us as desperadoes and levellers'.[18] The true enemy, according to Lovett, was the traditional one: 'KINGCRAFT, PRIESTCRAFT, AND LORDCRAFT'. But he felt that the middle classes too often displayed 'cupidity and selfishness'; in so doing, they made common cause with this enemy. Slowly Lovett began to modify his view of the middle classes. Yet he remained convinced that collective self-advancement rather than collaboration was the preferred route to victory. The poor must not allow themselves to be placed at the mercy of a 'few capitalists' or powerful groups of landowners. Organisation, based on enlightenment, was crucial to them. He had stated eloquently as early as 1831: 'I belong to a class of men who have been plunged into the depths of poverty – I sympathise with them in their feelings.' His views on this subject were not to change for almost twenty years.

Thus William Lovett was a bundle of political contradictions as he moved into the next and most famous phase of his life –

the agitation for the People's Charter. He had faith both in education and the capacity for individual advancement. He believed in the efficacy of economic co-operation, though with weight given to political instead of economic reform. He abjured violence or a challenge to the law which might lead to a disruption of the political structure, such as the widely-canvassed proposal of Benbow and other reformers in the 1830s for a people's convention to write a constitution for the nation. Yet Lovett vigorously supported the illegal unstamped press and revelled in working-class group identity. These cross-currents of radicalism defined his emerging career. They made him an interesting, perhaps a deeper man, than some of his admirers were prepared to admit.

3 The beginnings of Chartism

During the years 1836 to 1838 Lovett emerged as a major leader of radical reform. He founded the Working Men's Association (popularly referred to as the London Working Men's Association), one of the more important organisations of the early nineteenth century dedicated to the political and educational improvement of the working classes. He helped to draft the People's Charter, which gave a unifying dimension to the Chartist movement. He provided a stimulus to the development of provincial working-class associations. He wrote a series of tracts and pamphlets in which he presented impressive arguments for reform. He enunciated a programme of international co-operation among working-class radicals which foreshadowed subsequent activities in this area. That Lovett did all of these things at a time when his health was uncertain and he was struggling to make ends meet financially makes his achievements even more impressive. Those who regard him as an exemplar of rational politics focus with good reason on these years.

Still, Lovett's contribution to reform must be set within its proper context. Hovell, Tawney, Cole, and other earlier chroniclers of Chartism assume a dichotomy between advocates of moral and physical force. The former group, with Lovett as its purported spokesman and with a strong artisan base in London, is conceived to have been predominant at the outset of the movement. On the other hand, Feargus O'Connor, who built a mass following in the North of England, is perceived by this earlier group of historians as the chief advocate of physical force. According to this view, the divisions between the two men were focused in their respective organisations: the LWMA and O'Connor's National Charter Association, established in July 1840. Then, according to this interpretation, amid the excitement of monster petitions to Parliament in 1839 and 1842, numbers began to supplant reasoned argument as a political force. Lovett was believed to have lost most of his influence, while O'Connor gained an undeserved reputation as the strong man of Chartism.

To some extent, this traditional account of the early history of Chartism continues to be valid. In the late 1830s Lovett and O'Connor participated in an intense rivalry, and they gave differing emphases to their points of view and organisations. Their bases of support were, respectively, in London and the North of England. Lovett was on the whole the more moderate of the two men. He more often condemned the use of 'physical force' and violence, whereas O'Connor (at least until 1840) was more inclined to advocate it, if only for rhetorical purposes. Yet recent studies of Chartism by Epstein, Prothero, and Dorothy Thompson among others, have made clear the need to modify this picture. Without diminishing in any significant way the role of Lovett, who helped to initiate, encourage, and give form to several of the crucial political events of these years, it is evident that his following was relatively small and confined mostly to groups of skilled workers in the capital, who were not typical of the working classes. From 1836 to 1838 the LWMA was one of the leading radical organisations in London but it was not necessarily dominant. There were rival groups in existence, including the London Democratic Association, founded by George Julian Harney in August 1838, which drew its inspiration from the 'Jacobin' political tradition of the 1790s. And outside the capital many other Chartist associations began to form (including many affiliated with the LWMA) and to skirmish for positions of influence.

The years from 1836 to 1838 were a period of considerable

flux in radical politics. Chartism was a complex phenomenon. It incorporated strands of Owenism and trade unionism, together with a demographic mix of artisans, factory workers, handloom weavers, and disaffected outworkers. It had social and religious dimensions which blurred its political focus. It articulated class feelings in ways that cut deeply and involved even leisure and churchgoing activities. Lovett was one of several leaders who gave Chartism its shape; and arguably, by his emphasis on education, he was the most farsighted of its spokesmen. Yet the limited extent of his influence and the contradictions both in his own thought and in the Chartist movement at large must be kept in mind when assessing his role.

Much has been written about the LWMA, including accounts which draw extensively upon archival material in the Francis Place collection. But there are still aspects of its history that require clarification. One such area concerns the precise manner in which it came into existence in June 1836. What has been established beyond doubt is the importance of Lovett's close ties with the newspaper repeal campaign, especially the two committees he served as secretary: the 1834 committee to pay off the fines of Hetherington and Cleave; and Dr Black's 'Association of Working Men to Procure a Cheap and Honest Press', dating from the spring of 1836. Both associations were strongly influenced by Francis Place, with whom Lovett developed a close working arrangement during these years.

Contrasting explanations as to the relationship between these committees and the birth of the LWMA have been used to underscore political interpretations of Chartism. Place's version (supported by the historian D. J. Rowe) is that he and Dr Black were responsible for the founding of the LWMA. It was, he maintains, a product of their joint influence over the small group of artisans, including Lovett, who belonged to the two repeal organisations. By means of middle-class tutelage, these craftsmen were induced to abandon their wilder ideas and to concentrate on educational reform as a primary goal. In Rowe's words, 'the motivation and initial organisation of the working men came from this middle-class source, and . . . this influence continued to work behind the scenes'.[1]

Lovett (backed by Mark Hovell) is more discreet in his version of this event. He concedes there was a link between the repeal committees and the LWMA. But he gives little credit to Dr Black and none at all to Place for the establishment of the LWMA, stating only that 'a goodly number of active and influential working, persons who had principally done the work of our late committee'[2] were involved. The difference in emphasis is not unimportant. For if Lovett is correct, the primary stimulus of Chartism in London is seen to derive from the disaffected poor themselves. And subsequent accusations that Lovett was in the pocket of Place or was a closet 'Malthusian' (alluding to Place's endorsement of birth control) are difficult to sustain.

A reading of the archival material does not give a decisive victory to either side. There are ambiguities in the evidence, chiefly because Place is not always a reliable witness and because little is known about the history of the committees. Yet the weight of psychological probability is on Lovett's side. Even during this formative period of his life he was a sturdily independent man. It seems likely that he took what he wanted from both repeal organisations (which he dominated), making out of them what he chose. And what he chose was to create an organisation – the LWMA – not concerned solely, or even primarily, with the remaining penny tax on newspapers but with broader issues of political and educational reform.

By June 1836 the LWMA had supplanted the Association of Working Men to Procure a Cheap and Honest Press. Neither Place nor Black were significantly involved with the new group, although the former attended many of its weekly discussion sessions up to the spring of 1837. At the same time Lovett clearly rejected the Place/Black version of political economy, with its emphasis on natural economic laws and individual mobility. Instead he pursued his own more collectivist approach based on Owenite ideas. His prospectus for the organisation in June 1836, with its call for working-class unity and co-operation, has an authentic ring to it. Simultaneously, Lovett gave up his efforts to establish a reading room and coffee shop, with which Place had assisted him. He contributed books and furniture to the LWMA, housed in rooms in Upper North Place off Gray's Inn Road. For the immediate future his personal biography was intimately connected with that of the organisation.

The structure of the LWMA is of considerable interest because it closely reflects Lovett's thinking. Curiously, the LWMA was both a democratic organisation, which was its intention in political terms, and an elitist one, which is how its critics viewed it. Whereas O'Connor established various organisations beginning with his Universal Suffrage Club in July 1836 on the basis of an open membership and a high entrance fee, Lovett sought to recruit 'quality'. He conceived of the LWMA as a small discussion society meeting for purposes of general mental improvement. Only workingmen who showed themselves to be 'honest, sober, moral, and thinking' were to be allowed to join the association. Lovett wanted to draw them away from the 'tap-room', so as to fund 'a political school of self-instruction among them, in which they should accustom themselves to examine great *social and political* principles'.[3] Members of the LWMA were recruited by nomination and an initial screening process. If approved by three-quarters of the members, nominees were invited to join the society in return for a monthly fee of 1s. Lovett reluctantly agreed to a change in the membership rules in January 1839; henceforth, workingmen who subscribed to the principles of the organisation, and were proposed and seconded, would be accepted. Even with this change, however, the size of the LWMA never exceeded several hundred, while not surprisingly, most of its members had been active in the Owenite and trade union movements and in the newspaper repeal campaign. Considering its small size, the LWMA may be regarded as one of the significant pressure groups of the early Victorian period.

Lovett's conception of the organisation was interesting in yet another way. The LWMA consisted of working-class members 'as far as practicable'. Non-working-class participants – 'gentlemen radicals' like O'Connor and Robert Owen – were elected to honorary memberships. But they coud not exercise voting rights and, in theory, were not allowed to play an active role in the society. Thus feelings of class solidarity, muted in some of the theoretical pronouncements of the LWMA, underpinned its formal existence. Precedents existed for this, beginning with the London Corresponding Society in the 1790s, whose artisan membership supported political democracy, and extending to the more recent example of the National Union of the Working Classes. But the LWMA adhered consistently to the notion of a formalised class structure. And it did so amid pressure – acknowledged by Lovett – to 'co-operate with all those who seek to promote the happiness of the multitude'.[4]

The multiple activities of the organisation are a testament to Lovett's impressive administrative abilities. He was its secretary and, as such, responsible for almost everything it did. Unlike the NUWC, the LWMA was not divided into classes or study groups. Its membership met as a whole once or twice weekly to discuss current issues or to attend lectures and public readings. Formal decisions were taken by majority consent at quarterly meetings, with the entire membership of the organisation expected to be present. An executive committee, dominated by Lovett, conducted the day-to-day business of the organisation. But because of the small membership it seems to have been less important than in other organisations. Periodically the LWMA summoned public meetings for the purpose of circulating petitions and drafting political resolutions. Such meetings were usually held at popular radical locales like the Crown and Anchor Tavern in the Strand or the White Conduit House tavern in Islington. Attendance occasionally exceeded that of the full membership because radical reformers from all parts of London were encouraged to attend and the meetings were well advertised.

The LWMA did not publish a newspaper (though it did issue five numbers of a gazette in 1839), and it was not identified with one, unlike the NUWC, which had ties to Hetherington's *Poor Man's Guardian*. Yet Lovett, in his role as secretary of the organisation, rapidly established himself as a master of the penny tract. Beginning with the *Rotten House of Commons*, which was circulated towards the end of 1836, the LWMA published many pamphlets, mostly written by Lovett, with titles like *Address on the Subject of National Education* (1837), *Address to the People of Canada* (1837), and *Radical Reformers of England, Scotland, and Wales, to the Irish People* (1838). These tracts deal with subjects like economic distress, international solidarity, education, deteriorating conditions in Ireland, and, above all, the need for universal suffrage. The customary practice was to distribute several hundred copies of the pamphlets among the members of the LWMA and other interested reformers, though sometimes the numbers were higher. Subcommittees were set up by the executive committee to investigate problems or amass information about a subject which might then form the basis of a tract.

Invariably, it was Lovett who did the heavy work behind the scenes and put together the final draft of the pamphlet. He also spoke frequently at both the weekly discussion sessions and the less frequent public meetings. However, his most effective contribution to radicalism was as an unobtrusive polemicist who marshalled facts and arguments with care. Unlike O'Connor or

George Julian Harney, the able editor of several Chartist news-papers, Lovett never paraded flashy oratorical or journalistic skills. He was a technician, not a showman. But in the late 1830s, he produced a series of impressively crafted pamphlets, in which logic almost always got the upper hand over passion.

As secretary of the LWMA, Lovett engaged in other activities. He met frequently with sympathetic MPs, organised deputations to the government to complain about its policies, and directed the work of subcommittees, which were inquiring into such things as the conditions of work of London shoemakers and the lack of cheap housing in London's East End. The LWMA main-tained a steady drumbeat for reform for nearly three years. It expanded its activities beyond London, though not signficantly so. As a result of legal restrictions dating from the 1790s, it could not establish itself as a co-ordinated central body. But from the spring of 1837 onwards, 'missionaries' who included Hetherington, Cleave, and Henry Vincent, a vibrant orator, helped groups of workingmen in provincial towns and cities to establish local branches of the LWMA, which were technically independent of the London body. About 150 of these associations came into existence and served the useful purpose of strengthen-ing Lovett's image as a national leader. In reality, though, the bulk of his support remained concentrated in London, especially in the districts in and around Clerkenwell and Tottenham Court Road, where many politically conscious artisans resided.

What did the LWMA attempt to achieve? What were its goals? How radical was it? In one sense, obviously, the LWMA reflected a continuing evolution in working-class politics. Most of its mem-bers had previously worked with Lovett, including Hetherington, Cleave, and Robert Hartwell, a compositor active in radical causes who became a close personal friend. These men all believed in the long-term economic reorganisation of society and, in varying degrees, distrusted the competitive economic system with its inequalities of privilege and power. Yet to the exclusion of almost everything else, they emphasised the importance of education and politics. In part this was an outcome of the unstamped press campaign with its focus upon ideas. But it also resulted from a disillusionment with 'conventional' reform, which that event had helped to produce.

Members of the LWMA mistrusted the Whigs, whom they considered to be 'moneyed men'. When the Whig Reform Act of 1832 was passed, Lovett and his associates believed that no fundamental shift of political power had taken place. In their view the new political system too closely resembled the old one, notwithstanding many protestations of good intent. Moreover, they felt that the workers had been betrayed again in 1836 by the grudging compromise of a penny tax on newspapers in place of outright repeal. These events seemed to make clear the futility of any alliance with the middle class. Thus, Lovett and his colleagues decided to initiate a political offensive and assert the autonomy of working-class demands.

For most activists in the LWMA, political reform was the necessary lever of radical change. In the absence of a democratic franchise, they believed it unlikely that meaningful improvements would be carried out. Lovett and his associates contended that the most flagrant abuse was 'exclusive and corrupt government', which had to be frontally attacked by means of a transformation of political power. Such a change would enable workingmen 'to probe social evils to their source, and to apply effective remedies to prevent, instead of unjust laws to punish'.[5] Unequal landholding was abhorrent to the LWMA, which adhered to the traditional Painite formulation of the 'old radicalism'. But although its tracts contain little that might be described as anticapitalist, 'money' was also condemned for its pretensions at neutrality. In the *Rotten House of Commons*, Lovett wrote: 'Will it give us more comforts, more leisure, less toil, and less of the wretchedness to which we are subjected, if *the power and empire of the wealthy be established on the wreck of title and privilege?*[6] Again and again in the addresses and pamphlets of the LWMA, Lovett attacked 'exclusive legislation' and 'exclusive interests'. He encouraged workingmen to challenge the innumerable corruptions of faction. In his view, a purified working class must take the lead in the struggle against oppression because 'an enlightened people never would submit to despotism'[7] and because it would 'raise up a social and political edifice founded on national enlightenment and justice'.[8]

Idealism was a component of these pronouncements. Lovett genuinely believed that political and social evils, notably wars, would disappear once education became widespread and universal suffrage was adopted. He was a thoroughgoing democrat in spirit and in political beliefs. And his convictions stretched all the way back to the revolutionary decade of the 1790s, through the post-Waterloo years of reformers like Cobbett and Sir Francis Burdett, to the political battles of the 1830s. In putting the case for radical reform, Lovett intermingled the experiences of memory and activism. Privileged groups had first to be destroyed. Then a reconstruction along rational lines would take place, with self-respect and mutual obligations being emphasised in a framework of collective politics.

In one strikingly effective speech at a public meeting sponsored by the LWMA in February 1837, where the drafting of a People's Charter was bruited about for the first time, Lovett articulated several of these themes. He attacked the 'power and monopoly of the few' with their ramifying abuses: 'war, glory, splendour, fame, spectacles, songs and every other brutalizing and degrading means the demon of evil could suggest'.[9] Ordinary people must be impelled to change things by asserting their political rights. This would lead to the dissemination of knowledge (free schools, a free press, the unhindered circulation of political ideas) and other economic and social reforms. Only in one sphere was

William Lovett

Lovett cautious, both at this meeting and as a general propagandist for the LWMA. He believed that religion was a personal matter. Although he gave voice privately (and occasionally in public) to deistic and anticlerical sentiments, he regarded the public discussion of theological issues as out of bounds. Even at the LWMA's weekly discussion meetings, where controversy was a virtual *sine qua non* of good fellowship, it was tacitly understood that theology was not a fit subject for debate. Almost certainly it would create disunity in the organisation. To make the point clear, Lovett insisted that the group's discussion sessions be held on Thursday evenings rather than Sundays.

A striking aspect of many of the LWMA pamphlets was the attention they gave to the theme of international solidarity. As Henry Weisser has pointed out, radical politics from the 1790s to the 1840s had a strongly international flavour. The LWMA built upon this tradition. Like other groups of reformers, it perceived the United States as a land of freedom where republican institutions established the foundation for a better society. According to Lovett, who held to this utopian vision of America, 'a throne is not a necessary appendage to a nation's greatness; . . . wars are not necessary, either to maintain dignity or to balance power; . . . liberty and property may be secured without police spies, or hirelings in armour . . .'.[10]

In pursuit of its internationalism, the LWMA initiated contacts with reformers abroad, especially in France where two revolutions had been 'betrayed' in the previous half-century. Fraternal addresses and greetings were exchanged with French, Belgian, Polish, and Canadian reformers. In each instance, a call for political emancipation was intermixed with attacks upon specific abuses. The issue of Canadian self-government attracted particular attention because it involved colonial policy. In 1837, force was used to put down an insurrection by radicals in Canada who were demanding that elections be held for the executive and legislative branches of the government. This led to public meetings in London and two *Addresses to the People of Canada*, published by the LWMA, in which Lovett praised the Canadians for resisting the 'despotic ordinances and tyrant mandates' of their oppressors. He condemned the immoral policies of the British government in Canada and called for a union of subject peoples to protest against the suppression of liberty. In supporting violence in Canada, Lovett fell back upon the political theories of Paine. The argument was the familiarly abstract one. The rights of the Canadian people had been overridden and their nation 'dissolved into its original elements'. Bloodshed was therefore justifiable. Lovett's internationalist feelings prefigured his continuing interest in this subject. Subsequently he became a friend of the Italian nationalist, Giuseppe Mazzini, and participated in several associations which championed the rights of subject nationalities.

Notwithstanding his leadership of the LWMA, Lovett was constrained by his role as secretary. His language often seemed bureaucratic and he admitted that his expressed views did not always reflect his own thinking. But when he spoke in a non-official capacity at public meetings or wrote articles for radical newspapers, he expressed his feelings more robustly. Thus in the summer of 1836 he contributed five vehement letters to *Hetherington's Twopenny Dispatch*, a leading unstamped newspaper. His language was provocative, although his arguments were not notably different from what he had been saying for several years. Lovett singled out for castigation economic evils and the 'vultures who daily devour' the labour of the poor. He attacked political economists like Place for insisting that taxation and the Corn Laws, rather than economic and political privileges, were primarily responsible for inequalities. In these articles (which provide evidence that Lovett was not Place's lackey) he propounded Hodgskin's thesis: that the key to reformation lies in the recognition that 'surplus labour is at the mercy of surplus wealth'.

Lovett did not advocate force in these articles. But he hinted strongly that violence might be acceptable upon occasion because of the flagrant injustices of the system, which included 'infant sufferings and infant sacrifices' and the treatment of poor people as 'mere tools and instruments of production'. Lovett also suggested that private property might have to be brought under control. And in reaffirming, at least in part, his belief in economic co-operation, he attacked the prevailing system of self-interest, which allowed 'one man to engross for luxury what would suffice to make thousands happy'.[11]

Lovett's connection with the LWMA led to his best-known activity as a reformer, the drafting of the People's Charter. This document became the banner of the Chartist movement when it was adopted by a show of hands at a large public meeting in Glasgow in the spring of 1838. The Charter's six points (universal suffrage, annual parliaments, equal electoral districts, secret ballot, the payment of MPs, and no property qualifications for MPs) were presented in the form of a bill which, if enacted into law, would have immediately transformed Britain into a democracy. These demands went to the heart of the emerging movement because they enabled hundreds of thousands of scattered reformers to rally around a single focus for unity. All Chartists agreed on the six points, although many differed about the social and economic demands to be carried out in the aftermath of a political reformation. But with a unifying political symbol (and an economic/social programme in the form of a series of National Petitions) there could be no turning back. Much of the strength of Chartism, therefore, including its class cohesiveness, flowed from the Six Points.

Lovett's part in drafting the People's Charter was crucial although he was not the 'father of Chartism' (as is sometimes suggested) and was not singlehandedly responsible for composing the document. Credit must be shared with Francis Place and

John Arthur Roebuck, a radical MP who supported workingmen on many occasions in the 1830s and aided Lovett with some of his work in the LWMA. The origins of the Charter derive from a petition presented by the LWMA at a public meeting at the Crown and Anchor in February 1837. The petition incorporated the principle of universal suffrage (with women to be given the franchise as well as men) together with a justification for it written by Lovett. He claimed that Parliament had 'interests for the most part foreign or directly opposed to the true interests of the great body of the people', and that, since political rights were independent of social conventions, laws reflecting such interests were based on 'force or fraud'.[12] In support of the petition, in a speech described by the future Chartist leader, Bronterre O'Brien, as 'one of the most eloquent addresses I ever heard', Lovett urged workingmen to avoid being made 'machines and instruments of production'. He powerfully articulated the pride he felt in his humble origins: 'To hear a set of moustached debauchees wrangling for power and plunder talk of the people, one would suppose they were talking of so many sheep, which Providence has sent to be fleeced and devoured, instead of human beings'.[13]

Following upon the adoption of the petition, negotiations and meetings between representatives of the LWMA and sympathetic MPs were begun in an attempt to hammer out acceptable wording. These discussions dragged on for more than a year, in part because of the general election of 1837, which was caused by the death of William IV. Those MPs involved in the negotiations, in addition to Roebuck, included the prominent reformers Joseph Hume and T. Perronet Thompson. The spokesmen for the LWMA were all close associates of Lovett. They included Hetherington, Cleave, Watson, Vincent, and Richard Moore, a wood-carver who was highly regarded in radical artisan circles.

The drafting of a People's Charter was initially delegated to

Roebuck. But according to Lovett, the task was given over to him when Roebuck failed to complete his assignment on time. Lovett admits that he then asked Place to help him with the document but maintains that this is all Place did. For his part, Place claims to have essentially written the Charter when Lovett turned the work over to him. As with the comparable dispute about the origins of the LWMA, it is not possible to be certain which version is precisely correct. Lovett and Place were skilled at writing and both were capable of having formulated the wording of the Charter. What can be stated with a degree of assurance is that Lovett did the bulk of the work and, at the least, inspired the final draft, while Place, for his part, undoubtedly helped to polish it. Roebuck wrote the preamble to the Charter and Lovett then penned an address to accompany it in which he repeated the by now familiar argument that 'self government by representation' is the 'only true basis of Constitutional Rights' and that the enlightenment of the people, from which changes might be expected to flow, could be secured only by granting political power to them. In the final version of the Charter, universal suffrage was once again defined in its traditional form as encompassing only adult males.

The acceptance of the People's Charter in May 1838 officially launched the Chartist movement. At almost the same time the National Petition, demanding economic and political reforms, was drawn up by the revived Birmingham Political Union. Charter and petition gained support subsequently at a series of spectacular public meetings held in different parts of Britain in the spring and summer of 1838. Excitement was in the air. Outworkers and mill hands in the North joined hands fraternally with London artisans in a search for unity. It was agreed to assemble a convention in London early in 1839, which would insist upon the acceptance of the Charter. Within a short period of time the political situation had been transformed, in part due to the powerful efforts of Lovett during the preceding two years.

Before the assembling of a Chartist convention in February 1839, where he was to play a major part, Lovett was involved in an incident which affected his political future. Almost certainly he and Feargus O'Connor were likely to quarrel at some point. Both men had emerged as spokesmen for an incipient Chartist movement by the summer of 1838. Yet they had little in common other than their belief in the need for radical reform. O'Connor typified a blustering oratorical approach to popular politics; Lovett exhibited the inconsistencies and fine tuning of a mind that drew upon reserves of class feeling and self-reliance. Temperamentally O'Connor was an Irish romantic, Lovett a quietly-assured educator. Not surprisingly, many workingmen who found O'Connor's flamboyant style exciting (with its professed concern for the economic and social grievances of unskilled and semi-skilled workers) began to express disillusionment with Lovett. In March 1837 George Julian Harney and two associates resigned from the LWMA in dudgeon at Lovett's support of 'passive obedience and non-resistance' and his allegedly close ties with Place and Daniel O'Connell, the leader of the Irish repeal movement and a man whose radical sympathies were suspect. Harney subsequently founded the London Democratic Association, a rival to the LWMA, which advocated a more class-conscious approach to politics. In the same year Bronterre O'Brien broke with Lovett after a quarrel over the formation of the Central National Association, an organisation intended to elect radical candidates to Parliament by a show of hands at the hustings.

Still, it was the growing hostility between Lovett and O'Connor that created a belief in a physical/moral force dichotomy within Chartism and that helped to weaken the movement. Personal considerations were an important factor. The two men differed about ideas and tactics, yet in the late 1830s neither was an unvarnished exponent of a particular point of view. Both made compromises and occasionally said and did unexpected things. If anything, the 'moderate' Lovett was less willing to tolerate personal affronts than the 'extreme' O'Connor. A political marriage between them, even could it be brokered, was unlikely to be consummated.

But the permanent breach between Lovett and O'Connor (which was never patched together even on those few occasions when they temporarily agreed to bury the ideological hatchet) was caused by a specific incident occurring in 1838. It involved trade unionism, a subject Lovett was not deeply interested in. From 1832 to 1834, he somewhat tepidly supported attempts at general co-operative unions, including Owen's Grand National Consolidated Trades Union. He then participated in the mass demonstrations of March and April 1834 to protest the sentences of transportation meted out to the six 'Tolpuddle Martyrs' for attempting to establish an agricultural trade union. Lovett helped to raise subscriptions for their families and joined the Central Dorchester Committee, which publicised the incident. On the public platform and in several newspapers he defended trade unions, albeit in restrained terms. Trade unions, he claimed, were a means for resisting 'tyranny practised towards the workman'.[14] He was a member of the London Society of Cabinet-Makers, which performed some functions in common with trade unions, and served as president for a time. But to passionate advocates of trade unions, his views were perceived as decidedly lacking in emotion.

In 1837, a bitter strike erupted in Glasgow involving the cotton spinners. Violence ensued and a blackleg was murdered. Five leaders of the Cotton Spinners' Association were brought to trial on a variety of charges and found guilty only of the comparatively minor offence of picketing with intent to intimidate. Nonetheless, they were sentenced to seven years' transportation. This incident was treated by reformers like that of the Dorchester labourers (although the convicted men were not sent to Australia and were pardoned in 1840), with supporters of the union demanding an inquiry into the events as a way of discrediting the government. Daniel O'Connell, a quondam ally of trade unionists, turned decisively against them. He moved successfuly for a Select Committee whose brief was to investigate trade combinations in general. However, his true aim was to curtail the activities of trade unionists in Dublin. Many reformers became overtly hostile to O'Connell. They refused to have anything to do with the committee in the belief that it would lead to the reintroduction of the Combination Acts, repealed in 1824. Working-class and middle-class reformers engaged in bitter recriminations about these events.

In the midst of these altercations, Lovett, in March 1838, was appointed to the paid position of secretary to the London Trades' Committee, whose purpose was to scrutinise the activities of O'Connell's committee. Lovett was given this appointment at the behest of Place, who was once more in his old form as a parliamentary string-puller, and he held the position until April 1839, when the committee was wound up. In his work as secretary, Lovett was assisted by Place to correspond with trade unions throughout the country and prepare witnesses to testify before the committee. Both men sought to counteract O'Connell's hostility to trade unions. Place had little faith in the effectiveness of unions to improve economic conditions, believing that the laws of political economy would neutralise them. But he endorsed the workingmen's right to organise peacefully and opposed legal restrictions on them.

Lovett agreed with some of Place's views, asserting in an address published in March 1838 that 'there is a point beyond which we cannot force our wages'. However, as on previous occasions, he made clear his independence from Place. He attacked O'Connell in harsh language although the two men had worked closely together the previous year in the LWMA. Lovett maintained that the purposes of the Select Committee were to achieve 'cheapened labour, and for discrediting the people'.[15] He asserted that trade unions were a useful step in the collective organisation of respectable workingmen. Without them, the poor would almost certainly be reduced to an earlier state of economic degradation. Furthermore, it was unfair to contemplate restrictions on the activities of unions as long as other combinations were permitted, including 'the exclusive monopoly of law-making between peers and ten-pounders' and 'trades' unions among lawyers'.[16] Lovett accepted reluctantly that some Scottish trade unionists had perpetrated acts of violence and deserved punishment. But he attempted to justify these physical outbursts on the ground that the spinners had been unduly provoked.

Given Lovett's generally sympathetic views about trade unions, O'Connor's blistering condemnation of him in the *Northern Star* in February 1838 was somewhat unexpected. According to O'Connor, who broke with O'Connell over Irish policy and other issues in 1836, Lovett was being deceitful. He had conspired with Place and O'Connell to bring the Select Committee into existence, knowing that it would harm the workers. Almost certainly, since these charges were without foundation, O'Connor deliberately initiated this battle with Lovett at a time and place of his own choosing. He must therefore bear a large portion of the blame for undermining a potential working relationship between the two men. Yet Lovett, once goaded, was inconsolable. He responded with a sarcastic riposte, which came to be much quoted (and admired) by his supporters. O'Connor, he maintained, was the 'great "I AM" of politics, the great personification of Radicalism. . .'.[17] The ironic labels stuck. They wounded O'Connor, who retorted mockingly that 'I do more real work in a week than (Lovett and his friends) perform in a year!'[18] He insisted that Lovett was a close ally of O'Connell, whom he described as the 'masters' exclusive advocate'.

By the autumn of 1838 Chartism was gaining momentum, while at the same time the relationship between two of its leading spokesmen was sharply deteriorating. The tenuous unity of the movement – just being forged – was already beginning to dissolve over personal as well as ideological differences. As thousands of reformers assembled in different sections of the country to prepare for the forthcoming convention, Lovett defended himself vigorously against attacks by O'Connor and his allies, and in so doing began to define his position in somewhat more moderate terms. Amid the confusion of events, he took a strongly 'constitutionalist' line (that is, on the side of legality and against violence) while O'Connor implied that he was ready to use force whenever the situation warranted it.

A direct confrontation between the two men occurred in September when the LWMA convened the largest public meeting in its history at Palace Yard, Westminster, to choose delegates to the convention in London. Lovett made a temperate speech. He proffered the opinion that political power 'belongs to all, and should be exercised for the benefit of all'.[19] No single group possessed a monopoly of benevolence, he claimed, including the working class; but it was imperative that the latter not be deprived of any opportunity for self-improvement. He expounded a relatively mild criticism of the economic system, maintaining that there were good capitalists as well as 'mercenery and oppressive' ones. He also affirmed without equivocation that 'the mass of people seek not violence or commotion, but peaceable and orderly changes'. He made no reference, as he had on other occasions, to provocation as a rationale for violent measures. Most of the other speakers took a much harder line, including O'Connor, who proclaimed his willingness to 'lead the people to death or glory should I see the constitution violated'.[20] It is clear that the two men hated each other from the time of this meeting. According to Lovett, O'Connor was replaying the role of Benbow in the early 1830s, when the latter's advocacy of a general strike and of violence (as on the 'Fast Day') had helped to undermine the NUWC. The analogy with Benbow is unfair to O'Connor who, despite his occasional bombastic oratory, could be every bit as 'moderate' as Lovett. But both men were locked into personal and political attitudes which left them little room for manoeuvre.

By the end of the year Lovett's position became significantly weaker. He was jeered at several public meetings for attacking O'Connor and Joseph Rayner Stephens, a powerful though erratic speaker who was leading the popular opposition to the New Poor Law of 1834. 'Muskets are not what are wanted', Lovett stated at one meeting, 'but education and schooling of the working people'. He described poor law repeal, a key demand of many northern workingmen because of the harshness with which a system of workhouse relief was being imposed, as at best a 'partial grievance', a view which fostered the belief that he was subservient to Place and other political economists who supported the poor law. At a crowded gathering at the Owenite 'Hall of Science' in London, which was packed with O'Connorites, Lovett reiterated his opposition to violence: 'If they were willing to push onward in a reasonable endeavour to arouse the moral and mental energies of the people, he would be one of them; he was one of them in heart; but if there was to be any arming, any fighting, he was not one of them.'[21] As preparations for the convention accelerated, with Lovett, Hetherington, Vincent, Cleave, and Hartwell among the eight delegates selected to represent London, disunity appeared to be increasing. Numbers were clearly not on the side of Lovett and his friends, who in effect were challenging some of the oratorical and physical strengths of northern Chartism. Attention now shifted to the convention, which assembled in London in February 1839.

4 *A turning point in his career*

For the history of Chartism 1839 was a critical year and, in a sense, the same was true of Lovett's life. Both the historical event and the man developed along parallel lines before diverging in significant ways. For Chartism, 1839 was a year of unity followed by fragmentation and a temporary shift towards violent means. Lovett, on the other hand, continued to be transformed into an advocate of moderation, although for much of the time his views were not notably different from those of the more militant Chartists. With the advantage of hindsight, it is possible to see movement and man simultaneously reaching a high-water mark in 1839 before beginning a slow political recession and a reformulation of activities and tactics.

Throughout the late summer and autumn of 1838, Chartism had crystallised around the Six Points and the National Petition. Both documents articulated the political and economic grievances of the working classes and set into motion waves of local and national enthusiasm. For many poor people radical reform seemed a realistic possibility for the first time. In the words of O'Connor, as reported in his *Northern Star*: 'Out of the exercise of that judgement which belonged exclusively to the working class, a union would arise, and from that union, a moral power would be created, sufficient to establish the rights of the poor man . . .'.[1] And why not? Crowds of workingmen were being mobilised in West Riding textile towns and Lancashire factory districts on behalf of a cause that seemed to have unstoppable momentum behind it. Even in London, the outpouring of sentiment at the

Palace yard meeting in September appeared to betoken a break-through into mass politics.

The General Convention of the Industrious Classes (or 'People's Parliament'), which met in February at the British Coffee House in Charing Cross and then a few days later moved to rooms in Fleet Street, was to be the engine of this success. It was anticipated that it would pressure the government into accepting Charter *and* petition. Tactics were fluid. Yet a general strategy was agreed: to unleash concentrated moral power against the Whig government and force it to act if it refused to do so voluntarily. The Convention was a major incident in the history of nineteenth-century radicalism although, as Terry Parsinnen has shown, a long history of theorising about 'anti-parliaments' preceded it, beginning in the 1770s and later incorporating the activities of the NUWC and other groups in the 1830s. As in other instances, the organisers of the Convention wanted to bring about fundamental political changes by means of a quasi-formal 'constitutional' body.

Its history was stormy. In May it moved to Birmingham, where it adopted an extreme statement of views known as the Manifesto of Ulterior Motives. Several delegates were involved in rioting in that city's Bull Ring in July, which enabled opponents of Chartism to tar the Convention with the brush of seditious and violent behaviour. In August, the remaining members (now meeting again in London) dithered over whether or not to initiate a general strike, or 'Sacred Month', to gain their political objectives. Such a projected strike aroused strong feelings because of the likelihood that it would lead to violence; six days before the delegates reluctantly agreed to commence a 'national holiday' on 12 August, it was aborted by order of the Convention. For all practical purposes, this signified the end of the body, which was formally disbanded in early September. Although it had few specific accomplishments to its credit, the Chartist Convention represents an exciting chapter in British working-class history because of the avenues of change it seemed to open up. Yet in its closing stages, it degenerated into uncontrollable factionalism as a result of its conflicting aims and hopes.

Lovett's shifting fortunes mirrored those of the Convention. He was driven by the will to achieve a more just society, and in 1839 he worked towards this end with an almost superhuman intensity. He told the querulous Place, with whom he corresponded regularly at this time, that 'a great good will result from this convention'.[2] Lovett was involved in every detail of the body's activities and, to a significant extent, its sucesses and failures are a measure of his ability to shape events. At the end, there was much less to defend than he had hoped for. In personal terms, his inconsistencies had become so obvious that even his warmest admirers find it difficult to justify some of the things he did and said at the Convention. As secretary, he was guilty of administrative sloppiness, which his enemies used against him. And in August, in what must be adjudged a reprisal taken by the authorities against one of their more reasoned critics, he was tried and imprisoned for seditious libel and incarcerated for a year. When Lovett was released from Warwick Gaol twelve months later, the political landscape had changed decisively. His career, until then at a crossroads, began to move into a second stage in which education took primacy over political activism.

Before assessing Lovett's part in the Convention, it is necessary to clarify his personal standing. In her otherwise admirable history of Chartism, Dorothy Thompson misleadingly describes him as 'middle class'. In fact, Lovett may still be characterised as a struggling artisan in 1839, as he had been for fifteen or so years previously. If anything, his economic position had worsened in the previous decade. He was a journeyman cabinet-maker, in a trade that, by the 1830s, was under continual threat from 'dishonourable' elements within its ranks. Lovett never employed any workers on his own and hardly worked at all at his trade after 1836 because of intermittently poor health. He interspersed odd jobs with his political activities, in order to support his wife and daughter, with whom he lived in extremely modest circumstances. Early in the 1830s these accommodations had been in Greville Street, where Lovett combined Owenite and book selling activities; from 1836 on, he lived near Gray's Inn Road, in the house in which the LWMA was based and for which it paid him a small rental. To add to his store of financial difficulties, Lovett was personally hurt by a questionable venture he became involved with in 1840: the publication of the *Charter* newspaper.

Lovett's ideas in 1839 may be more legitimately characterised as 'middle class' than his economic position in the sense that, as Trygve Tholfsen and others have shown, respectability and propriety were indigenous to both craftsmen like him and to the middle classes. But until the 1840s, when his thinking underwent a third important shift, he remained wedded to the outlook of the poor. He was not of 'gentle' status like Feargus O'Connor or Henry Hunt, or well educated like Bronterre O'Brien, although all three men were more 'radical' than he was. On the contrary, Lovett struggled almost every day of his working life to earn an adequate income, while expending prodigious amounts of time on causes and organisations in which he believed. William Ellis became a modest benefactor in later years; yet Lovett had no truly wealthy patrons to sustain him, such as Julian Hibbert, who underwrote the activities of Carlile and James Watson. Whatever Lovett did he did singlehandedly, which strengthened his inner resources and helped him to define a sense of individualism.

Lovett has been accused of promoting factionalism at the Convention because of his continuing ties to the LWMA. Some historians (as well as contemporaries) have suggested that he brought an organisational base into the assembly and thereby contributed to its failure. The charge is unfair. In a technical way, Lovett's abilities created an 'organisation man' out of him because he possessed the skills of a first-rate secretary rather then of an orator or journalist. O'Connor controlled the influential *Northern Star*, founded in Leeds in November 1837, which gave him a commanding position in the Convention. George Julian Harney and Henry Vincent were Chartists with unusual oratorical powers, guaranteeing them access to enthusiastic public forums. Lovett had only a passion for detail, shorn as it was in this instance even of adequate support. Thus he clung tenaciously to the LWMA, an organisation he had nurtured for three years and which, by 1839, was in a process of disintegration. Still, he was not a man of faction, and when the Convention assembled, he virtually dissolved his organisation by urging its members to join the new Chartist associations being formed in London and elsewhere. However various the contradictions defining Lovett's character, he spoke with an independent mind. He was often imprecise about his goals and fuzzy as to the best means for legitimating them. Yet he had as much, if not more, integrity as any other Chartist leader, O'Connor included. This much must be stated in his defence before considering a more serious and accurate charge: that his activities during this critical year bore little resemblance to his later professed ideals.

As in its sections dealing with the early 1830s, Lovett's *Life and Struggles* expounds the thesis that he continually sparred with 'extremists' at the Convention. According to this somewhat dubious interpretation of events, the body was doomed from the start because of the 'violence and folly' of a 'few mad advisers' who appealed unrestrainedly to the 'passions of the multitude, [and] stirred up the demons of hate, prejudice, and discord . . .'.[3] Almost certainly, Lovett tells us, the Convention would have been 'unmarked by violence and untarnished by folly' if it had not been for 'the violent ravings about physical force' of O'Connor and his cronies, who 'scared (the middle class) from our ranks'.[4]

Lovett distinguishes between the 'prudent portion' of the group led by himself and other serious artisans, and 'hot-heads' who prated insistently about the need for 'ulterior measures', including insurrectionary violence.

This sanitised reworking of Chartist history, which is also uncritically accepted by some historians, is misleading with reference to Lovett *and* O'Connor. Both men demonstrated a lack of consistency in the face of fluctuating circumstances. Neither openly countenanced violence, yet they refused to condemn it outright. There were, to be sure, important shades of difference between them. O'Connor was often indiscreet in his choice of words, while Lovett, eschewing violence, also more frequently expressed his preference for lawful and prudent methods of agitation. Yet on the key issues taken up by the Convention – support for the Manifesto of Ulterior Measures; whether or not to move the body to Birmingham where, presumably, it would be able to express its sentiments more forthrightly; and most significant, whether to endorse a general strike – both men reacted inconsistently, sometimes illogically. The situation in 1839 was fluid. Lovett and O'Connor responded to events quickly; at the same time, they felt an antipathy for each other. Not until after the dissolution of the Convention, when they faced lengthy prison terms for their activities, did their tactical and strategic commitments harden – and then in divergent ways.

Lovett was chosen secretary at the outset of the Convention in February, and he held this position until he began to serve his prison term in August, when he was briefly succeeded by his wife and then by Robert Lowery. According to a journalist's sketch, Lovett seemed to look the part of a secretary. He was 'tall, gentlemanly-looking . . . with a high and ample forehead, a pale, contemplative cast of countenance, dark-brown hair, and . . . a very prepossessing exterior'.[5] He was also nervous and taciturn, a pair of traits commented upon by almost all those who knew him. Yet notwithstanding his physical 'inoffensiveness' and obvious qualifications for the task, there was some opposition to Lovett from O'Connor's adherents. Bronterre O'Brien voiced the doubts of this group when he maintained that a visible role for Lovett at the Convention would detract from its unity. Still, after an extended debate he withdrew his negative motion, and Lovett was chosen unanimously to fill the unpaid position of secretary.

The job proved to be more demanding than anything he had done previously and, in some ways, it represents as impressive a contribution to working-class history by Lovett as his leadership of the LWMA. He did all the paperwork for the assembly without an infrastructure to aid him. He corresponded with Chartists in different parts of the country, oversaw the work of 'missionaries' like Vincent, and organised the collection of a National Rent subscribed to by local Chartists to defray the expenses of delegates and underwrite other expenditures of the body. Lovett took the minutes at every formal meeting of the Convention, meaning three or four times weekly. He drafted the body's official statements, including very probably its controversial Manifesto of Ulterior Measures. He communicated policy to newspapers like the *Northern Star* and the *Charter*. And he kept up contacts with sympathetic MPs like Thomas Attwood and John Fielden, an essential activity, particularly in the early days of the Convention when it was hoped that both the petition and Charter might be adopted by the Commons. All of these things Lovett did without recompense (only his expenses were covered), while simultaneously representing London in the capacity of an ordinary delegate. He bore the complaints of his critics with equanimity, even when they charged him, unfairly, with partiality as well as inefficiency. Overall Lovett's performance was a confident one, which makes clear how effective quiet leadership can be in a highly charged political situation.

The debates of the delegates are a fascinating compendium of radical arguments during a time of great political excitement. The Chartist representatives analysed many of the controversial issues of the day, including an extension of the suffrage, free education, repeal of the poor law, and the need for reform in Ireland. They bewailed the existence of widespread poverty, especially among factory workers and handloom weavers. They deplored social and economic inequalities. They repeatedly called for political and other changes. Yet the most passionate discussions concerned the tactics to be used to gain their objectives, in the face of an overwhelmingly negative stance taken by the Melbourne government, the military and police forces of the country, and the majority of newspapers. From the beginning, therefore, delegates faced the likelihood of defeat. The petition, measuring three miles in length and including an estimated one and a quarter million signatures, was easily defeated in the Commons after a desultory debate. The Charter made even less progress. Several MPs, including Thomas Attwood (who presented the petition), refused to introduce it in its present form. Expectations weakened further when a cluster of moderate delegates from Birmingham, angered both by a lack of progress and the militant speeches of Harney and other Chartists, withdrew from the Convention.

By early spring, therefore, serious consideration was being given to 'ulterior measures', which might be adopted in the event of failure. Harney spoke for the insurrectionary left when he maintained that 'there is no argument like the sword – and a musket is answerable'.[6] Other delegates, such as R. J. Richardson of Manchester, endorsed this position. Adopting militancy as its tactic, the Convention approved a provocative *Address to the People of Great Britain and Ireland*, which was signed by Lovett. It included the following statement: 'If forced to the contemplation of physical force by the foolish extravagance of our rulers, if forced to resort to it in self-defence even to the last tribunal, we are prepared for the appeal rather than to continue in bondage, and rather to lay our heads upon the block as freemen than on the pillow as slaves.'[7] Place's reaction to the *Address* was predictable. He told Lovett that it was 'offensive to all but a *portion* of the working people and to that portion it was misleading'.[8]

More explicit than the *Address*, and among the most contentious acts of the Convention, was its Manifesto of Ulterior Measures, published in May, which Lovett put his signature to as secretary and which he seems to have written, although it basically summarised the deliberations of a small group of reformers (primarily Lovett's allies) who met informally at the Arundel Hotel in London. The Manifesto is not a statement of which Lovett, the retrospective chronicler, was proud. He describes it disingenuously in his *Life and Struggles* as an 'act of folly', and claims that he agreed to it to avoid splitting the body. 'I sacrificed much in that convention for the sake of unity', he observes. Lovett's explanation is partly convincing because he did make some personal sacrifices for unity. Yet more important, he had become a captive of the political enthusiasms of the time. Like O'Connor, he could see no way to resolve the political situation in the spring of 1839 other than by using rhetorical violence which might, conceivably, lead to physical force. As a correspondent expressed it in 1841: 'Moral force is but physical force in perspective; and it is this perspective coercion, ever becoming clearer and clearer, which alone makes oppressive rulers cease their oppression'.[9]

The Manifesto restated in its own terms the revolutionary dictum of Paine, which was a staple of popular radicalism. In essence it said the following: If the rights of the people continued to be ignored, they had an obligation to resort to 'ultimate' measures. In the 1830s, the NUWC had enunciated such a doctrine, and in a much more restrained way, so had the LWMA. But the language of the Manifesto was unusually blunt. Lovett contended (assuming that the precise words are his) that the 'GOVERNMENT OF ENGLAND IS A DESPOTISM AND HER INDUSTRIOUS MILLIONS SLAVES' and that the people must awake from their 'political slumber'. This need not necessarily involve 'wild revenge' on their part; but (in a finely drawn distinction) they must cease to be passive beings 'who can witness [their] country's degradation, without a struggle to prevent it'.[10] Invoking the political war chant to be made famous by O'Connor and militant orators like Joseph Rayner Stephens, Lovett warned the oppressors of the poor that the latter would utimately prevail, 'peaceably if we may, forcibly if we must'. Six potential courses of action were then outlined by him: the withdrawal of funds from savings banks, the conversion of paper into gold or silver, a general strike of one month, armed defence against injustice, the application of pressure to candidates for parliament who 'consider themselves veritable representatives of the people', and exclusive dealing with Chartists (meaning a boycott of shop-keepers whose political credentials were insufficiently radical). Subsequently the Convention agreed that 'simultaneous meetings' should be held in different sections of the country to determine which of the six courses of action was best.

The Manifesto of Ulterior Measures generated opposition among some Chartists, although not, as might have been supposed, from Lovett or the 'moderates' thought to be in his camp. O'Brien, for example, unexpectedly denounced it as too extreme in its endorsement of violence. He urged that it be privately circulated, a position rejected by the Convention, which decided to publish 10,000 copies for immediate distribution. Likewise, O'Connor urged the delegates to follow a policy of caution. He persuaded them not to take a vote on the Manifesto until after the Convention moved to Birmingham, which it did at the beginning of May. Lovett, on the other hand, characterised the statement as 'straight-forward and manly'. He urged that it be discussed prior to a change of venue; otherwise the actions of the Chartists would be construed as 'cowardice'. He also declared that the Manifesto represented 'the spirit of Englishmen, the suffering millions of Great Britain [who] . . . would rise against the systematic oppression under which the working classes were morally and politically degraded'.[11] This tough rhetoric, difficult to square with the conventional interpretation of Lovett as an advocate of constitutionalism and 'moral force' Chartism, laid him open to O'Connor's subsequent accusation – ironical in light of their future disagreements – that he was the concocter of a 'violent measure'.

The debate on the Manifesto revolved primarily around tactics, and recent work by historians has necessitated a rethinking in this area. James Epstein observes that the Chartists were in a quandary because their movement was a revolutionary one in a constitutionalist setting. He is right in the sense that violent acts could not be overtly condoned by men who professed, as did Lovett and O'Connor, to be law-abiding. Yet, it was clear that basic concessions were not going to be won by traditional means. Minor reforms might possibly be gained in several economic or administrative areas. But before a radical restructuring of the political system took place, the authorities would have to be cowed, at least verbally, or so a large number of Chartists reluctantly began to believe.

Lovett seems not to have fully understood the ambiguous interaction between illegality and violence, at least in 1839, and the same was likely true for O'Connor. Both men (and many other reformers involved in radical politics in the first half of the nineteenth century) were engaged in a game of political bluff. They accepted the need for intimidation short of force: a rhetorical intimidation considered as a threat, not a reality. In other words, the People's Charter would be 'won' if their bluff was successful. Otherwise, as proved to be the case, the majority of

Chartists would probably choose to cut and run. O'Connor waffled over this point several times and his reputation suffered as a result. When Lovett also engaged in rhetorical excess, his inconsistencies were tidily overlooked, or excused by Tawney as a 'weapon of defence', or, less convincingly, paraded before sympathetic readers and historians as an example of conscience. Special pleading adds little to our understanding of Lovett. The truth is that advocates of both 'moral' and 'physical' force (whether or not these are useful descriptive terms) often found it possible to move in varying paths, depending upon circumstances and the harsh, if sometimes unpredictable, responses of those in authority.

Lovett's defence against accusations that he supported the proposed Chartist general strike in the summer of 1839 is more convincing than his justification for the Manifesto. For one thing, the idea of such a strike was identified with William Benbow, his sworn enemy since the 'Fast Day' incident of 1832. According to Benbow, who first proposed a 'Grand National Holiday' in the early 1830s, all workers were to agree to halt their labour for a month to enforce their political demands. This proposal was incorporated into Chartist tactics, though not necessarily as a practicable course of action. Many Chartists, including Lovett, while willing to contemplate illegal tactics, rejected the possibility of violence held out by a strike. Yet the idea gained substantial support in the Convention and was one of the six modes of action presented in the Manifesto of Ulterior Measures (with the interesting proviso that the strikers had to agree to abstain from drink).

Lovett never publicly approved the 'sacred month' and privately he made his reservations known. He suggested that if the Convention agreed to a strike, one or two of the better organised trades be called out initially. After this limited ploy proved successful, which Lovett doubted, the remainder of the workforce would cease their labour. He later maintained that this proposal was intended to kill the scheme because he knew that a strike would not gain sufficient support. He would therefore be in the happy position of negating an unacceptably radical plan by means of an act of 'kindness'.

Lovett's second line of defence is more persuasive: that is, when the Convention tepidly endorsed the general strike in July, he was safely ensconced in Warwick Gaol. Thus he avoided making a public decision, which almost certainly he would have been compelled to do if still secretary. In any case, the attempt to launch a strike was a fiasco. In early August, O'Connor attacked it as a 'wild and visionary scheme' and the Convention declared it to be 'utterly impracticable'. It was cancelled before it could be carried into effect. Lovett therefore managed to preserve his reputation as a 'fluid' moderate, and, in later years, to condemn with good conscience the unjustified behaviour of his opponents.

His work as secretary ended abruptly in July when charges of sedition were brought against him by the Birmingham authorities. In the late spring of 1839, the Melbourne government began to take resolute action against the Chartists. Several thousand were arrested between 1839 and 1841, including most of the leadership; of this number about 470 were convicted and imprisoned. Action on such a scale effectively undermined the movement. Prison created opportunities for publicity and martyrdom. But at the same time it removed activists from political settings and sometimes broke the spirit of resolute men. Conditions in Victorian prisons were rigorous, even though some Chartist prisoners (O'Connor in York Castle, Stephens in Chester Castle) were treated with comparative leniency. Those emerging after a lengthy period of incarceration were frequently more malleable and willing to compromise than when they went in.

Even at a time when political prosecutions remained commonplace, the charges brought against Lovett are unjust. The accusations against him were part of a general attack upon the Convention: symbolic rather than substantive. The circumstances were as follows: early in July some Birmingham magistrates forcibly suppressed a public meeting in the Bull Ring, which was held without a permit. London's detested 'new police' were called in to do the deed, and disturbances occurred, leading to the use of troops. As secretary of the convention, Lovett signed three resolutions condemning the suppression of the original meeting (not the ensuing riots), which were distributed in the form of a placard. These resolutions charged the magistrates with a 'wanton, flagrant, and unjust outrage' against the rights of the people. According to Lovett they had made invidious distinctions between rich and poor; similar meetings of protest by middle-class reformers, he pointed out, had been allowed on many occasions. For putting his name to this document – an act described by Mark Hovell as heroic – Lovett and John Collins, a delegate from Birmingham who took the placard to the printer, were arrested and charged wth seditious libel for 'unlawfully contriving and intending to disturb the public peace, and to raise discontent in the minds of the subjects . . .'.[12]

The trial of Lovett and Collins is among the more celebrated events of the Chartist period. They were imprisoned initially in Warwick Gaol for nine days before being freed on bail. Then, in August, they were brought to trial at the Warwick Assizes. A National Defence Fund was established for them, and the Chartist press publicised their case, which was unexpected considering that many other Chartists were being apprehended at the time and events in the Convention were rushing towards an unsatisfactory climax. At several public meetings physical force was bruited about as a possible tactic to be used against the government if Lovett and Collins were convicted. Lovett rejected such talk, but at one meeting (between the time of his release on bail and his trial) he spoke passionately about the 'brutality and blood thirsty disposition of the Metropolitan Police and the injustice of the authorities in allowing those men to act as they did against the people, without the necessary forms of law having been complied with'.[13]

The trial itself was less dramatic than anticipated. It resembled the usual format of political trials: first, a speech by the Attorney-General accusing Lovett of intending to 'bring the law into disrepute' during times of 'turbulence and insubordination'; then a riposte by Lovett, defending himself, in which he made a reasoned case against the prosecution; finally, a published version of the trial by Hetherington which brought in some needed money. Lovett's trial was held immediately after the conviction of Collins (who was represented by a barrister), making the chances of his acquittal extremely unlikely. Still, he made a good try at winning the case. His oratory lacked distinction but he spoke with considerable emotional resonance and energy.

'Seditious libel' was a vague offence used to silence critics of the government. It was not easily defended against because it rested on obscure provisions of common law, particularly recondite to a defendant untrained in the law. Lovett took a moderate position at his trial, as if to contrast his demeanour with the harshness of the government. Speaking before a packed courtroom, he denounced all 'violent and criminal modes of redress', including the Birmingham riots. He maintained that he had personally never been present at a tumultuous assembly in the Bull Ring or anywhere else for that matter, and was being prosecuted solely because of his choice of words. At worst, Lovett pleaded guilty to a 'public censure of a public act', which, he admitted readily, he would do again. According to him, the law had to be as accessible to the poor as it was to the rich; it must not be used to serve the partial interests of privileged classes. The jury took less than three minutes to reject these arguments and find him guilty of seditious libel. He and Collins were sentenced to one year of imprisonment in Warwick Gaol.

Lovett's case received considerable attention from the press and Parliament, in part because of the poor treatment he received while a prisoner. It was common practice to treat political prisoners as debtors, an example being Richard Carlile, who was incarcerated in Dorchester Prison for six years in the 1820s. Debtors could spend their own money on provisions and writing supplies and had unlimited visiting privileges. In such circumstances prison might offer the possibility of a cathartic experience, notwithstanding its discomforts, which included poor food, a lack of heating, inadequate sanitary facilities, and prolonged mental isolation. The temperament of a 'victim' might be needed to turn it to advantage. But this was at least a possibility.

For Lovett the possibility did not exist. Conditions in Warwick Gaol were terrible, and the Home Secretary, Lord John Russell, refused to countenance any improvement, probably because he wished to make an example of the Chartists, who were coming to be identified with violent acts like the armed uprising in Newport, Wales, in November 1839, led by John Frost. Lovett was not a good candidate for prison. His health had been poor for several years. In prison he suffered from bronchial and intestinal disorders. He did not possess the psychology of a 'victim' who was prepared to absorb punishment for the sake of a political cause. Rather, he was depressed about his treatment without, seemingly, being able to muster the inner resources to capitalise on it. Lovett could not easily bear separation from his wife, who was only allowed to visit him twice during the year and, as a result of financial difficulties, had to leave their Gray's Inn Road home.

He resented being classified as a felon. He was angry that his claims to respectability were ignored and that he was confined with 'common criminals' (technically misdemeanants) who in his view lacked a sense of moral justice. Lovett could not abide the gruel, potatoes, and bread, which composed the bulk of his diet. After protests by Henry Warburton, William Molesworth, and other radical MPs, and the incessant efforts of Place behind the scenes, his regimen was modestly improved. He was given cold bacon and tea regularly, as well as paper and writing implements. Mary Lovett sent him tracts and books to read (mostly noncontroversial), while Place, anxious to gain a convert to political economy, forwarded volumes of Ricardo and J. R. McCullough, which Lovett read, though not, as he put it, 'to much advantage'. Partly because of these improved conditions, Lovett began to use his days in prison more productively. In the spring of 1840, he and Collins wrote *Chartism*, an influential book which was published after their release and made a powerful case for educational and moral reform.

It is difficult not to feel sympathy for Lovett, particularly because of his adamant refusal to be bound for good behaviour in exchange for a remission of his sentence. He kept up a drumbeat of protest throughout the year. He petitioned Parliament several times and wrote numerous letters to his wife and Place describing the conditions of prison life. Like other political prisoners, he experienced brief periods of depression intermixed with elation. For example, in January 1840, he admitted that 'taking previous circumstances into account our condition is much improved'.[14] Yet essentially, he never reconciled himself to his incarceration. He felt abandoned by many Chartists with whom he had worked closely in the Convention. For several months after his imprisonment began, they raised funds and tried to sustain a public interest in his case. Subscriptions were collected for him and Collins by trade unionists and Chartists, and Mary Lovett was supported financially to some extent while he was in prison. Yet as an increasing number of Chartists began to be prosecuted and convicted, allies of Lovett, like Watson and Hetherington, lost ground to more militant reformers. As a result, his cause generated less publicity.

He became disenchanted with radical politics and, in his own mind, began to reconstruct the history of the Convention. Prison marks a fault line in Lovett's life because his first consistent development towards a 'moral force' position dates from this experience. At his trial he had emphasised his belief in legal and non-violent methods of resistance, which were linked in turn to the position he had taken in the autumn and winter of 1838 when under attack from O'Connor. His book *Chartism* further dramatically accentuated this shift. Henceforth, Lovett may be characterised as an exponent of moderate tactics who favoured educational reform as a complement to political change. He continued to be a vigorous spokesman for the poor, but in a tempered way that made his views acceptable to some middle-class reformers. In 1842 Lovett was to reach out to these middle-class reformers publicly for the first time. This would probably have happened even without the experience of prison because of his increasing disillusionment with political agitation, and, even more so, because of his intense dislike of O'Connor. But his year in Warwick Gaol exacerbated these feelings, giving psychological as well as intellectual ballast to his moral approach to political issues.

One final event in Lovett's life at this time is significant in his development. This was his involvement with the weekly *Charter*, a newspaper commenced in January 1839. The *Charter* publicised and supported the workingmen's cause and became the official organ of the Convention. Its prospectus was issued in September 1838, while Lovett was still secretary of the London Trades' Committee. At the instigation of William Carpenter, his associate in the LWMA and a professional journalist who became the first editor of the paper, Lovett was appointed secretary of a committee to manage the newspaper. It was a co-operative venture involving representatives of the LWMA, London trade unionists, and members of other political organisations. Blocs of workers were given control of the paper in exchange for their financial support. As one of the *Charter*'s three trustees, Lovett incurred a liability for its debts; when it became mired in difficulties in 1840, he found himself encumbered with debts of more then £60. These were paid off by subscription but the incident severely unnerved him. He began to articulate a scepticism about the efficacy of group politics. He vowed to keep clear of journalism in future, a pledge he did not keep. 'This I think will sicken me of all newspapers,' he dejectedly told Place, 'and of being again responsible for the proceedings of a committee.'[15]

By 1840, Lovett was at the mid-point of his life. He had turned an important political corner and was to acquire an increasing reputation for integrity and moderation. The next few years were to witness a more precise definition of his faith in working-class education and politics. He was to rely less than before upon organisation and to eschew mass support. At the same time, his leadership of reform in this middle period of his life, which lasted from 1840 to 1847, was to possess a consistency and vision it had previously lacked.

5 *The moral and social regeneration of the people*

During the thirty months from July 1840, when Lovett was freed from Warwick Gaol, to December 1842, when his attempt at an alliance with middle-class reformers ended in failure, he articulated some central themes of Victorian respectability. Education and moral improvement became primary concerns for him. He attempted to define an 'alternative' working-class culture – rooted in artisanal attitudes and not self-consciously political – which was based on an ethos of self-help. At the same time, he became marginalised from politics. Chartism, although in decline after the heady days of the late 1830s, continued to dominate popular radicalism. In emphasising individualism, Lovett was increasingly out of step with its leading ideas. Likewise, in his strenuous efforts at class collaboration, he began to opt for a liberal rather than a collectivist approach to politics.

When Lovett left Warwick Gaol on July 25th, he was 'considerably emaciated' and had difficulty walking. In its final months, prison had proved nearly unendurable for him. He had complained unceasingly about its physical and mental rigours. Feeling disconsolate about the immediate future, he needed to escape for a time from the pressure of group politics. As with other radical reformers who had been incarcerated for substantial periods of time (Hunt, Carlile, and O'Connor are examples), he oscillated between hope and pessimism. Upon his release, the latter mood predominated. He deplored the selfishness of the middle classes, while scoffing at the 'ignorance and prejudices of the multitude'.[1] It was essential, Lovett firmly believed, to stitch together another movement for the reformation of abuses. But this would take several years; for the time being he would wait upon events and assess the impact on the working classes of *Chartism*, the book he and Collins had written in prison.

Lovett was not a man to hesitate before taking a decision. Sometimes he was inconsistent about political options because events beyond his control propelled him in conflicting directions. Yet invariably he knew what he wanted. Before returning to Newlyn for three months of recuperation with a brother who lived there, he made several important decisions. One was to give up cabinet-making permanently. Lovett had never derived much pleasure from his trade, which had been thrust upon him out of necessity when he was an adolescent. Nowhere in his writings does he reflect with satisfaction upon the creative fulfilment that skilled labour is supposed ideally to provide. Furthermore, he had earned little money from cabinet-making and, as David Goodway points out in his study of London Chartism, the prospects for improvement in this trade were limited. Having rejected an offer from Samuel Smiles to work with him as an editor on the radical *Leeds Times*, Lovett decided to become a bookseller instead. He leased a room in Tottenham Court Road and began to prepare for his new line of work, which he had dabbled in for several years in the 1830s as the owner of a reading room and small circulating library. Bookselling provided him with a minimal income, however, and for the remainder of his life he struggled to earn money in two additional ways: via paid secretaryships and, from 1849 on, by teaching. He also began to accept financial assistance from better-off reformers, a common practice among working-class radicals in the nineteenth century though one to which Lovett, with his sensitivity and self-respect, did not take readily.

He re-entered the world of radical politics feeling increased bitterness towards O'Connor. Lovett was by temperament á man of restraint although not, in personal terms, a forgiving one. In his view O'Connor, the 'great I AM of politics', continued to be an obstacle to human enlightenment and rational reform. He could not brook this situation lightly and was determined to change it. At the same time, while denigrating violence (and, more strikingly, illegality) in the clearest possible terms, Lovett staunchly reaffirmed his class loyalties. The continuing political crisis in the nation and Lovett's own involvement with it make evident the potential contradictions in such a position.

Lovett's increased moderation led to an important decision. Shortly after his release from prison, he decided to skip a meeting in his honour in Birmingham, which Collins attended, allegedly for reasons of health but in reality because he had heard that 'extremists' were planning to be there. He chose instead to appear at a huge banquet in Islington presided over by Thomas Wakley, the MP for Finsbury, where he felt certain 'prudent men and women' would predominate. Among the latter were Hetherington, Watson, Cleave, and Richard Moore, Lovett loyalists who were preparing to wage a battle against the 'physical force' Chartism they felt O'Connor represented. Lovett enjoined those present at the meeting (he was never reticent about this) to remain faithful to the People's Charter with its Six Points, even if they felt the need to make other short-term compromises. Political democracy was still his vade-mecum, his justification for political involvement. It alone would assure 'the formation of a Parliament composed of good men of all classes, who would at once proceed to mitigate the evils of poverty and oppression, and devise the means by which prosperity and happiness should soon gladden the face of our fertile land'.[2] All else – repeal of the Poor Law, for example, which many Chartists were demanding, or repeal of the Corn Laws, a leading objective of middle-class reformers – were 'partial', if desirable, improvements. At the banquet, Lovett also reaffirmed his commitment to peaceful methods of agitation. Such methods, he believed, were likely to be successful and worthy of self-respect.

A final significant decision taken by Lovett (not yet shared with his public) was to offer a hand of friendship to middle-class reformers. This was by no means an inevitable political course, as some of his admirers have suggested. To poor reformers, the middle classes had proved unreliable from the early 1830s on, most recently by their implicit support for the rejection of Chartist demands. Lovett had distrusted them for many years and continued to regard them as ruthless in their pursuit of an unequal sharing of power. Still, they might be useful collaborators, so long as they were prepared to accept his principles. It is essential to understand Lovett's position at this time because he has been accused by Goodway and others of being 'class collaborationist'. In fact, his political goals in the early 1840s were consistent with those of the previous decade: in essence to keep the struggle for a democratic franchise alive and to win significant educational and other reforms for workingmen. He and O'Connor agreed on these points. Their disagreements continued primarily to be tactical, with Lovett in personal terms being the more unyielding of the two men. In different ways both men are heroic figures in working-class history.

Lovett's resoluteness is best seen in his relations with Place. These were close, even intimate, in the early 1840s. The two men wrote to each other frequently. They saw each other a great deal in private. Lovett owed a debt to Place for his solicitude and assistance while he was in prison. But despite some public signs to the contrary, he refused to adopt as his own Place's rather crabbed view of radical politics. Unlike Carlile in the 1820s, Lovett was not an easy mark for the propaganda of political economy. He did not become a convert to this ideology until

1847, and then it was William Ellis who inspired him rather than Place. Nor did Lovett concur with Place's sour analyses of the Convention. The latter body, Lovett insisted, had done some good, in spite of its tendencies towards 'pot-house politics'; it had at times been overly aggressive but, in its own way, had promoted the dignity and welfare of working people.

Lovett also made clear that Place's population theories, with their endorsement of artificial methods of contraception, were not to his taste. He was prepared to read with an open mind tracts Place sent him expounding these ideas. But he would not underwrite them except in general terms in so far as they strengthened the case for reform. According to Lovett, the economic system was producing unacceptable distress among poor people. The way to eradicate this distress, however, was not by population control or the working of 'natural economic laws' (which were the favoured methods of the political economists). On the contrary, class action was necessary because such evils were artificially created. Thus in his correspondence with Place, Lovett continued to urge the claims of workingmen and the need for radical reform, starting with the People's Charter. He was not an 'aristocrat of labour' or, as yet, a Victorian liberal. Even his calls for moral regeneration were not especially to Place's liking, though clearly preferable to O'Connor's approach.

In October 1840, while Lovett was still recuperating in Cornwall, *Chartism* was published. He had wanted it to be circulated immediately upon his release from prison but Place, who did some of the editing and financed the book, held it up until textual changes could be agreed upon. Although *Chartism* sold only a few thousand copies, it went through two editions and initiated significant changes in Lovett's life. Technically it was a work of collaboration with John Collins, a minor 'Christian Chartist' from Birmingham. Yet it is difficult to perceive what Collins's contribution consisted of other than some passages extolling temperance and moral improvement. The leading ideas appear to have evolved from Lovett's previous writings for the LWMA (1837-38), particularly two addresses he had written entitled *To the Working Classes of America* and *On Education* and a petition on national education. These exhorted the need for a collective effort to promote enlightenment and free general education, 'not as charity, BUT AS A RIGHT, a right derivable from society itself'.[3] Although conventional in structure and reminiscent of earlier Owenite educational proposals, with its environmentalist approach, *Chartism* remains one of the odder literary products of the period. It is part political tract, part educational nostrum, part specific blueprint for the National Association for the Political and Social Improvement of the People, an organisation that was to replace the LWMA and its affiliated bodies, which by 1840 had virtually disappeared. *Chartism* also signifies Lovett's commitment to education as a goal complementing radical reform, and which, increasingly, was to become in his mind the chief means of achieving the moral improvement of the people.

In the political sections of *Chartism*, Lovett took the usual pot shots at O'Connor and his allies because of their alleged predilection to 'talk violently or behave unjustly'.[4] Yet he expressed hope for the future. He maintained that the improving segment of the working classes must keep up its task of regeneration and 'create and extend an enlightened public opinion in favour of the People's Charter'. In doing so, it would accomplish three objectives: 'to place our institutions on the basis of justice, to secure labour its reward and merit its fruits, and to purify the heart and rectify the conduct of all, by knowledge, morality, and love of freedom'.[5] Thus Lovett regarded authentic working-class action as crucial to the political, economic, and educational aspirations of the British people. In this sense, *Chartism* merely amplified statements he had made earlier in the name of the LWMA. But to a greater extent, it emphasised the component of moral force ('recent experience has greatly served to lessen the faith of the most sanguine in their theory of force'[6]), while warning those resisting change that they faced a 'frenzied and desolating position'.

The passages in *Chartism* dealing with education are striking. Here Lovett sketched out his proposals in detail. In *On Education* (1837), he had urged governmental support for a comprehensive school system, including the use of public funds. Fearful of the dangers of state control, however, he had argued the need to create democratically-elected school committees to provide separate educational tiers. These tiers would range from infant schools to colleges, with the latter enabling adults to study science, politics, architecture, and other of the 'highest branches of knowledge'. Lovett was adamant that religious teaching must be excluded from the schools. It would thwart their chief function, which was to dilute sectarian feeling and promote a 'spirit of brotherhood'.

Yet as impressive as *On Education* was, it conceived of the educational process as part of a conventional jigsaw puzzle in which the key pieces remained political. In *Chartism*, however, the balance began to shift decisively towards education itself, which, in a memorable act of self-assertion, was to be fostered by the people. They would promote their own emancipation and, as well, bring about a series of 'glorious' mental and moral changes for the benefit alike of women and men, poor and rich, discontented and powerful. An effusive optimism characterises the educational sections of *Chartism*, as Lovett and Collins grope for a rational solution to human problems. Too little had been achieved so far because of ignorance. Now, they asserted, the people must be roused to a grand scheme of moral and social regeneration.

The educational proposals in *Chartism* were intended to create a multi-level school system, including Infant, Preparatory, and High Schools, as well as adult classes and circulating libraries.

Chartism touched upon methods of teaching children (it favoured the Pestallozian technique of instruction by means of objects). But Lovett was more interested in adult education with its self-improving features. Evening instruction would cheer the industrious classes after their lengthy hours of toil and prevent the formation of 'vicious and intoxicating habits'. Likewise, productive labourers would acquire useful skills in vocational schools, where prospective farmers, teachers, and manual workers were to be trained. None of these schemes, according to Lovett, should be teased into existence with the aid of the state. Nor was there a place for philanthropic activity. On the contrary, schools were to be self-supporting institutions, financed by the 'aggregate pence' of the poor. If everybody who signed the National Petition of 1839 agreed to contribute a penny weekly, Lovett claimed, more than eighty schools annually could be built together with hundreds of libraries.

What gave a political dimension to *Chartism* was Lovett's suggested mechanism for carrying out its educational ideas. In some ways the proposed National Association resembled the LWMA. For example, both organisations combined political and educational functions. But whereas the latter looked to the conventional political devices of petitioning and passing resolutions to achieve its educational ends, Lovett conceived of the NA as 'accumulating means of instruction and amusement' for the millions, and 'morally training fathers, mothers, and children to know their rights and perform their duties'.[7] Furthermore, the LWMA had not promoted many cultural activities, whereas the NA was to 'devise sources of enjoyments' for its members. Alcohol was to be rigorously excluded from its premises because it encouraged irrational behaviour. But not music or dance. Music, if carefully nurtured, would encourage habits of virtue and morality; dance, 'among the social recreations in which both sexes can participate',[8] might usefully meld elements of physical and mental gratification. As Brian Harrison has suggested in another context, the encouragement of social and cultural activities by reformers like Lovett exemplified the Victorian respect for both 'nature' and respectability. Like the Owenites, with their halls of science and social festivals, Lovett was trying to have it both ways: to fuse discipline with pleasure into a distinctive commitment to improvement. Thus *Chartism* signified his shift away from conventional political activism towards a rationalism which, in psychological terms, appears to have been shaped by the isolation of prison and, more speculatively, by a perceived loss of political influence.

The dissolution of the convention and the imprisonment of its leaders had weakened Chartism. Local organisations, shorn of their leaders, began to dissolve in late 1839. Others became a shell of their former selves. Many Chartists remained active in trade societies, local WMAs, Democratic Associations, political reform societies, and reading and improvement clubs. But the movement lost some of its national focus. Only the *Northern Star* and a few other Chartist newspapers sustained the cohesiveness that had been won in the spring and summer of 1839, a cohesiveness to which Lovett had contributed substantially. By the summer of 1840, with O'Connor still in prison (he was released from York Castle thirteen months later), the situation began to improve. New Chartist activities and organisations emerged and new strategies were devised. In July an effort at a national organisation was commenced in the form of the National Charter Association, basically an O'Connorite organisation. Local NCAs soon began to supplant most other organisations. In October five NCAs existed; by the time of the convening of a second National Convention in April 1842, there were forty-three; by 1845, the total membership of the NCAs probably approached 40,000. A degree of unity – more tenuous than previously – was re-established, primarily as a result of O'Connor's leadership.

To the extent that it is meaningful to interpret Chartism after 1840 in the light of a presumed 'physical force/moral force' dichotomy, the NCAs were closer to the former position. They were more combative than the WMAs had been and looked to the aggressive *Northern Star* for a lead. But as James Epstein makes clear in his study of O'Connor, the latter had rational political goals: in essence to lead a unified working-class movement. The same thing is broadly true of Lovett. Both reformers championed the interests of the working classes by means of their respective organisations; neither enjoyed a monopoly of virtue or 'moderation'. But with the experiences of prison informing their attitudes, the tactics of each man diverged. For O'Connor, the Charter (and the package of social and economic reforms it stood for, including repeal of the Poor Law) could be won by mustering numbers and by a combination of solid organisation and rousing platform oratory, as foreshadowed in the Convention of 1839. For Lovett, success depended increasingly upon workingmen who were committed to personal improvement as well as collective reform. Given this divergence of views and O'Connor's overwhelming superiority in numbers, it is evident why he regarded Lovett's proposals in *Chartism* as a challenge to the unity of the movement. Lovett's refusal to join the NCA when invited to do so (on the dubious ground that it was illegal) exacerbated the tension between the two men. He and O'Connor, antagonistic since 1838, continued to move along irreconcilable lines.

The break became final in March 1841 with Lovett's 'New Move'. In that month he and seventy-three other reformers published an *Address to the Political and Social Reformers*, which was a call for the projected National Association (NA) to come into existence. Those joining Lovett in this initiative included many of his usual associates, among them Hetherington, Cleave, Watson, Moore, and Henry Vincent, a leading teetotaller. The *Address* established the case for the NA in bold political terms. It emphasised the connecton between reform and self-improvement. Its tone was vigorous. If the working people wanted to do away with 'class legislation' (this phrase was prevalent in Lovett's vocabulary for many years), they must, according to the *Address*, become their own 'SOCIAL AND POLITICAL REGENERATORS' and establish an institutional structure reflecting their interests. The People's Charter continued to be the essential means to this end, and it had to be gained as soon as possible. But an apparatus of 'social and moral displays' (schools, libraries, tracts, cultural functions) was an invaluable auxiliary in the struggle. By emphasising the need to win these goals through 'sobriety and moral culture', the *Address* implied that education might eventually supplant political reform in importance (although it remained unclear how precisely this reversal of objectives was to take place). Following upon the suggestion made in *Chartism*, the *Address* also called for weekly penny subscriptions to establish the schools and libararies that would make the new organisation a success.

On paper the *Address* was an admirable call to arms. Yet predictably, O'Connor and his followers did not see it that way. They struck back forcefully in the pages of the *Northern Star*, seeking to forestall the creation of the NA. They derisively labelled Lovett and his followers 'Knowledge Chartists', an accusation that caused R. H. Tawney many years later to observe caustically that in 1841 'the brains had gone out of Chartism'.[9] What was implied by the launching of the NA – and O'Connor understood this – was the possibility of an alliance between the new organisation and the middle classes, a scheme that was to be essayed in the form of the Complete Suffrage Movement. O'Connor, who was himself not averse to an alliance wth the lower middle class provided it could be accomplished on his terms, nonetheless wildly asserted that Daniel O'Connell, Joseph Hume, and other parliamentary reformers were behind Lovett's proposal and, more plausibly, that the 'real object of the new move was to destroy the old move'.[10] In fact his repeated attacks upon the NA were intended to be pre-emptive.

Lovett's New Move created a major division among the Chartists, in part because he was accused of canvassing for support in secret. Several original signatories to the *Address*, such as Edmund Stallwood, a veteran radical journalist, insisted that their names be deleted after pressure was applied by O'Connor (admittedly, Lovett published the seventy-three names without their specific approval). On the other hand, Charles Neesom joined the NA because, he claimed, he would not give in to intimidation. Charges and countercharges were exchanged between supporters and opponents of the New Move in the spring and summer of 1841. At a London rally one speaker called for Lovett's assassination. For his part Lovett claimed that O'Connor's 'tools and dupes' were trying to destroy him because he would not accede to their clumsy efforts to dominate London politics. O'Connor's rebuttal took the form of an assertion that powerful factions, Whigs and Malthusians included, were using Lovett to fracture the solidity of the working-class movement.

In political terms, Lovett could not win this battle with O'Connor. He had neither the numbers nor the institutional resources to do it. Nor, very probably, the political will. His erstwhile colleague, John Cleave, the publisher of the *English Chartist Circular* and many Chartist tracts, broke with him and defected to the NCA. The *Northern Star* was irredeemably hostile. Most Chartist organisations were affiliated with, or effectively branches of, the NCA, and therefore antipathetic to Lovett's New Move. On the local level, Chartism continued to be as complex a phenomenon as before. Temperance advocates, secularists, Owenites, political radicals, practicing Christians, anti-Poor Law agitators, land reformers: all played a part in the movement. But in so far as *national* symbols were important (and they were), the division

87

was relatively straightforward. Lovett and a small number of supporters stood on one side of a fissure labelled 'moral force' or 'Knowledge Chartism', in a loose alliance with groups of temperance reformers and 'Christian Chartists'; on the other side was poised the numerical weight of O'Connor. The struggle was an unequal one, although this does not mean, as David Goodway contends, that Lovett had become an insignificant figure in working-class politics. Far from it, as events were to show.

The National Association for the Promotion of the Political and Social Improvement of the People was officially launched in the autumn of 1841 and it survived until 1849. Its educational and cultural activities will be more fully discussed in Chapter six. However, as a political rival to the NCA, it proved ineffectual. Its membership never exceeded 500, and of that number some were female 'auxiliaries', that is, wives and daughters of members. In theory, as prefigured in *Chartism*, the NA was open to persons of all 'CREEDS, CLASSES, AND OPINIONS' who supported the political and social improvement of the people, including a sprinkling of middle-class reformers like W. H. Ashurst. In practice, most of its members were artisans: associates of Lovett from the LWMA and the war of the unstamped, with a sprinkling of new recruits like W. J. Linton, the future author of the *English Republic*, and John H. Parry, who later became a prominent barrister.

The major political question confronting the NA was whether to support an alliance with the middle classes. By the spring and summer of 1842, Chartism had begun to revive appreciably. A second National Petition was being circulated with millions of signatures appended; there was increased support for Chartism in London; monster rallies were convened in the North of England; several new Chartist papers appeared; and industrial unrest in Lancashire and Yorkshire was becoming linked with political disaffection. Still, Chartism remained localised and its aspirations beyond the immediate goal of winning acceptance of the Six Points were fuzzy. Given this situation, some reformers believed that the success of Chartism depended upon an alliance with the middle classes. In their view, this great movement – without the support of men of influence and property – appeared doomed to having its petitions rejected and the demands of its supporters largely unmet.

Lovett came to accept this position and, with the backing of the NA, attempted to conclude an alliance with the middle classes. Before discussing his involvement with the Complete Suffrage Movement, his commitment to Chartist goals must once again be emphasised. To be sure, Lovett was becoming an educational reformer. He deplored the use of illegality and violence. He was not wholly sympathetic to social and industrial demands, such as repeal of the Poor Law, which he favoured but only as part of an overall political settlement. Yet his support for the People's Charter was not much different from O'Connor's. Admittedly, he now accepted that political change was not a panacea and that problems would remain even if the Charter was secured. 'Class distinctions', observed Lovett, could not be removed, 'in a day or a week, or even in six months'.[11] But principles were not subject to compromise and such principles for Lovett included, above all, fidelity to the Six Points. The NA affirmed, through its *National Association Gazette*, that 'the Charter and nothing but the Charter can be the basis of a union between working and middle classes'.[12] Other objectives must give way to this one, including the National Petition of 1842, which the NA rejected because it endorsed repeal of the union with Ireland, that 'darling crotchet of Irishmen'.[13] In place of the petition, the NA forwarded its own remonstrance to Parliament in 1843, encompassing educational and political goals and making clear its devotion to a democratic suffrage.

Still, Lovett was receptive to a deal with middle-class

reformers, and initial overtures came from the latter, notably Joseph Sturge, a Birmingham Quaker active in anti-slavery and other causes, and Edward Miall, who founded the *Nonconformist* in 1841. The goal of Sturge and Miall was to bring about a *rapprochement* between middle-class reformers and Chartists, above all, to fuse repeal of the Corn Laws with working-class demands for political democracy. The Complete Suffrage Movement, which was a product of this overture, is a milestone in radical history because it was one of the first serious efforts in the nineteenth century to bridge class differences as a way of advancing radical reform.

Perhaps an alliance with the middle classes *and* unswerving loyalty to the Charter, as favoured by Lovett, were incompatible goals. After all, the Charter was both symbol and text. As symbol it stood, in Surge's view, for 'improper and violent conduct', possibly a threat of revolution; whereas for Lovett and those in his camp, it encompassed a web of political and cultural experiences, including imprisonment, which were integral to working-class aspirations. Likewise there were textual problems: could the followers of Sturge and Miall be persuaded to endorse universal manhood suffrage? Could Lovett be induced to accept something less, perhaps a variant of household suffrage? In the final analysis, what did 'Complete Suffrage', a term invented by Sturge, mean? Was it substance without symbol? Symbol without substance? Or neither?

These ambiguities account in part for the breakdown of the Complete Suffrage Movement, although to Sturge, who was the most far-sighted of the middle-class radicals (O'Connor for one spoke in complimentary terms about him), 'Complete Suffrage' equalled substance. Sturge believed in class reconciliation and accepted the case for political democracy. Yet the symbol of the Charter was too much for him. Lovett represented symbol *and* text, even though to his discredit he fudged the distinction between the two on one critical occasion in 1842. The circumstances were generally unfavourable to him. Among other things, he had to cope with the strong opposition of O'Connor, who described Complete Suffrage as 'Complete Humbug'; with defections within the NA; and with a background of industrial unrest culminating in the trade union disturbances in the North during the summer months ('Plug Riots'), which Lovett condemned for their violence.

Lovett tried to walk a narrow line. In February 1842, he attended a meeting in London to plan for a Complete Suffrage conference to be held in Birmingham. With some reservations he put his name to an imprecisely-worded memorial drafted by Sturge calling for a 'fair, full, and free exercise of the elective franchise to which [the people] are entitled by the great principle of Christian equity, and also by the British Constitution . . .'.[14] Lovett believed that this indicated support for the Six Points; to show his good faith he endorsed Corn Law repeal, a measure he regarded as 'partial' at best. He worked industriously to prepare for the forthcoming conference, where the platform of the Complete Suffrage Union, founded in January, was to be fleshed out.

At the four-day conference in Birmingham in April, attended by about forty representatives of the working classes, Lovett firmly stood his ground. He described himself as a 'pledged man', telling the delegates that the Charter was the legislative 'text book of millions'. It must not be watered down, he stated, a position which caused the sceptical Miall to observe that the working classes were not acting 'quite the wisest and the most politic part for the accomplishment of their purposes'.[15] After an acrimonious debate, Lovett gained support for the *substance* of the Six Points. Yet, unexpectedly and perhaps unnecessarily, he compromised on its *symbolism*. With O'Connor's supporters not present to hold him to his purpose (the NCAs did not participate in the conference), he agreed to postpone a definitive

statement on the Charter until a second conference was convened. He has been much criticised for accepting this delay,
probably rightly so. The failure to resolve the status of the Charter
meant that disputes were certain to occur later, under less favourable circumstances as it turned out. But Lovett trusted Sturge
and genuinely believed he could win him and his associates over.

After the April conference, Lovett worked energetically to
make the Complete Suffrage Union a success. The stated aim of
the CSU was to keep up a public clamour for the 'great principle
of political equality'. Many of Lovett's associates joined the new
organisation, including Hetherington, Vincent, and Robert
Lowery. Some Chartists were members of both local NCAs and
the CSU, although O'Connor frowned on this. Bronterre O'Brien,
who was present at the April conference, endorsed Complete
Suffrage, somewhat surprisingly considering his radical reputation. Local CSU associations were formed and numerous meetings
held to promote class collaboration. The world of popular
radicalism was abuzz with activity. In the summer months, Sturge
unsuccessfully fought the parliamentary seat at Nottingham
against John Walter of *The Times* and received the support of the
Chartists, including those not affiliated with the CSU.

Lovett was a member of the Council of the latter organisation.
He helped to draft its *Address* and participated in many of its
meetings, including a large one held in London in August. He
travelled several times between London and Birmingham, an
unusual occurrence for a man who generally clung to the metropolis. During these months his theme, as enunciated particularly
in the *Address* of the CSU, was the need for reconciliation between
the classes. According to Lovett, this was a time of crisis in the
political affairs of the nation and it was urgent to establish a
'general bond of brotherhood' which would secure the 'political
and social deliverance of the country'. Middle-class radicals could
feel assured that the working classes had 'no ulterior object

inimical to the general welfare of society'.[16] The details of suffrage were yet to be worked out. But, Lovett observed, private property was 'sacred and inviolable, equally in the poor man's labour and the rich man's possessions . . .'.[17]

The three months prior to the convening of the second CSU conference in Birmingham were critical for Lovett and the putative middle/working-class alliance he supported. The NCAs agreed to send representatives to this conference and, in a series of battles for delegates, gained the upper hand over Lovett's supporters. Lovett believed that O'Connor's aim was to wreck the meeting. Half of the nearly 400 delegates were working-class (selected from separate lists by non-voters) and half middle-class (chosen by electors), and of the former an overwhelming majority were from O'Connor's faction. Even in London the NCAs won twenty-four places against three for the NA. Thus Lovett had only slim organisational backing at the December conference. He had to negotiate not only with middle-class delegates like Sturge and Miall, who were not entirely reconciled to his brand of radicalism, but with NCA representatives pledged to retain the 'Charter'. He had no room for political manoeuvre.

At the December conference, Lovett took an uncompromising stand on the Charter. He was furious at the tactics of the Sturge camp, which came to Birmingham intending to discuss a lengthy 'Bill of Rights' in its place. Lovett insisted that support for the Six Points had been agreed in April (as it had in general outline) and that the Chartists 'could not be parties to any compromise of their peaceable principles'.[18] In the key debate of the conference, he moved a crucial amendment, to wit, that the Charter, and it alone, be incorporated into the final statement of objectives. Amidst 'loud and continuous cheering', Lovett reaffirmed that the Charter formed 'the basis of the present agitation in favour of the suffrage', and that it had been 'well known amongst the public; they were wedded to it, and they could not be weaned from it'.[19] Therefore the Charter had an overriding claim to superiority over any other document. Friends and opponents of Lovett among those present agreed that the speech was the best of his career. But the middle-class delegates responded tepidly. One delegate stated that the CSU had not adopted the Charter: 'They did not, and they never would'. Miall pleaded with Lovett to accept the *substance* of political democracy, 'in whatever form it was offered, or under whatever names'. Lovett would not relent on this, partly because he had no alternative if he was to retain any authority within the Chartist movement; but also because as a matter of principle he was no more willing to compromise than O'Connor.

The highlight of the Birmingham meeting (and, in human terms, perhaps of the entire Chartist experience) occurred on the final day when O'Connor rose to endorse warmly Lovett's amendment. For a moment it seemed possible that the two antagonists might revive a working relationship and campaign once again under the same banner. Lovett spurned the embrace, demonstrating how antipathetic he felt towards O'Connor. By so doing, he cut himself off politically from both sides: from the CSU with whom he and his allies were, in the final analysis, unable to cut a deal; and from O'Connor, whom he continued to excoriate in extreme personal terms. With the latter's support, Lovett's amendment was carried by 193 to 94. But on the next day, Sturge and his group left the hall, to be followed afterwards by Lovett and his allies. Lovett would not work with O'Connor, nor would he merge the NA with the NCA, a proposal made by Thomas Cooper.

These days of personal symbolism, had Lovett known it, were to mark the effective end of his pretensions to lead the Chartist movement. He was but forty-two years of age. The remaining thirty-five years of his life were to be devoted to political activism on a diminished scale and, with unwavering enthusiasm, to moral and educational reforms. His period as a working-class agitator in the public spotlight was drawing to a close. Chartism continued to set a reduced political agenda until 1848, culminating in the presentation of a third National Petition and a monster rally on Kennington Common in March of that year. None of its political demands were accepted until a generation later. Class unity of the kind envisaged in 1842, that is, behind a democratic political and social agenda, remained a chimera. Middle-class reformers won their chief goal – Corn Law repeal – in 1846, and thereafter were less interested in an alliance with working-class radicals. To a degree, middle-class liberalism began to contend with radicalism as an ideology attractive to workingmen. Lovett's reputation grew after 1842, but largely in personal terms. His days as an initiator of events – even in quiet, bureaucratic ways – were at an end.

6 Peace and other issues

From 1842 to 1849 Lovett was preoccupied with the activities of the National Association. During these years he continued to canvass the possibility of an agreement with middle-class reformers and to attack O'Connor as unfit to lead the working classes. He became less of a spokesman for suffrage extension. He drifted away from the mainstream of Chartism, to re-emerge occasionally in cameo performances. More emphatically, he turned his blend of moral idealism and political radicalism into new paths: the peace movement, temperance, women's rights, above all, educational reform. In what, admittedly, was a situation of increasing political isolation, he had the satisfaction of remaining loyal to his beliefs. Like Robert Lowery, Henry Vincent, and other moderate Chartists, Lovett seemed (in the words of Brian Harrison) to evolve naturally into a 'thoroughly representative Victorian'.[1]

The National Association has been dismissed as a minor organisation, an 'impractical' debating club according to W. J. Linton, who belonged to it for a time and was sympathetic to its aims. Linton was right in terms of numbers. O'Connor's NCAs continued to make the running with sound political organisation and support from the Chartist press. In 1845, a Chartist Land Co-operative Company was established to promote O'Connor's plan to replace urban labour markets with groups of small landowners. Likewise, local trade unions flourished in the North side-by-side with co-operative associations, Chartist Churches, and political and freethinking associations. In such a setting, the NA counted for relatively little. It comprised a single group of reformers confined to London (its City of London branch became in effect the NA). Its activities were diffuse and not, seemingly, effective, consisting as they did of a small number of political meetings, the publication of tracts and a newspaper, and miscellaneous educational and social activities, many of them sparsely attended. Yet the NA warrants much closer analysis than it has received from historians because in many ways it mirrors the self-improving efforts of an important segment of the working classes at a time of bitterness and fragmentation.

Lovett was appointed secretary of the NA in April 1842, and he worked at this job until his resignation in November 1846. He received £1 weekly (not an insignificant sum for a man of his class) from July 1842 to December 1845, when his salary was increased to 35s. This constituted virtually all of his income during these years since his Tottenham Court Road bookshop, which he managed sporadically, yielded little money. Still, he gave his colleagues superb recompense for their investment. As secretary, Lovett did most of the work for the NA, as he had done for the LWMA. He composed its addresses and kept up a correspondence with local reformers, organised lectures and political debates, ran the NA's coffee room, and controlled the finances of the organisation, which were a constant source of anxiety. Lovett was, to be sure, not *the* NA. Some members of the organisation disagreed with him and were not hesitant to make their views known. They did not share his hostility to O'Connor and his distrust of mainstream Chartism. But his role was the dominant one. It is important to bear this in mind because recent historiography has tended to focus on the texture of the Chartist movement at the expense of its personality. Lovett, in spite of an unassuming style, was a man of formidable ability whose influence on matters of substance it is all too easy to overlook.

Lovett attended two sets of weekly meetings and kept minutes for each. One was the council of the NA, consisting of twelve members in addition to the secretary and treasurer. This group, which included Hetherington and for a time Collet D. Collet, Lovett's leading opponent in the organisation, dealt with general problems. It took decisions regarding political and cultural matters, established subcommittees to prepare reports, oversaw the activities of the National Hall in Holborn (which was the association's centrepiece), and initiated contacts with groups like the London Mechanics' Institute and the National Temperance League. The other body that met constantly was the committee empowered to run the National Hall. This committee was technically responsible to the council, although it usually acted independently. Lovett was one of four Directors of the Hall. Thus every aspect of the NA's activities, whether political, financial or social, passed through his hands. There were factions on both bodies. Yet, for the most part, Lovett managed to get his way.

His technique of exercising influence is an example of a skilled reformer at work. He belonged to almost all of the NA's subcommittees, frequently initiating proposals which were accepted or, if he did not have the votes, postponed for future discussion. His passion for parliamentary form was almost herculean. How otherwise could Lovett have continued week after week to participate in discussions about the most minute details of organisation: room rentals, admissions to events, hiring of lecturers, and so on. But he did – in the sanguine belief that this was the way to change a system that shunted workingmen aside and allowed primarily only for the expression of influence and privilege.

The leasing of a National Hall in July 1842, in Gate Street, Holborn (on what is now the corner of Kingsway), was an inspiriting event for Lovett and his supporters. Acquired for twenty-one years with the financial backing of middle-class reformers, this decaying structure was soon put into a proper state of repair. It consisted of several rooms and some galleries, which were set to use in a variety of ways. Other groups rivalled the NA in the 1840s in the range of their cultural and educational programmes, including the Owenite Hall of Science in Islington and the John Street Institution, founded in 1847, to which freethinkers were attracted. These bodies reflected aspects of an alternative working-class culture taking shape as the result of the interaction between reformist politics and educational mobility. But between 1842 and 1849 the National Hall was the central meeting place in London for working-class reformers who embodied self-improving aspirations. It did not always fulfil the exuberant intentions of its founders. Yet in the words of Richard Moore, a friend of Lovett for many years, it acted as a medium 'through which a sound rational nucleus of reformers might appeal to and gather strength from their fellow men, and by a reserved and tolerant deportment increase the good feeling already beginning to exist between the middle and working classes'.[2]

The NA published a small weekly newspaper, the *National Association Gazette*, funded by subscriptions from its members. This paper survived for seven months, beginning in January 1842, before expiring in a sea of financial problems. Its circulation was about 1,000 per number and it was hardly read outside the purlieus of the organisation. It had little to say to those not attuned to Lovett's ideas; indeed, its investors complained that many Chartist booksellers were refusing to stock it. However, the *Gazette* was edited with considerable panache by John Parry, a close friend of Lovett, and its political articles – particularly those espousing women's rights (the paper's masthead proclaimed: 'The Rights of Man and the Rights of Woman') – stated the official position of the organisation.

The cultural and social activities undertaken by the NA followed closely upon the ideas outlined in *Chartism*. Primarily because of Lovett's enthusiasm, these activities included dancing and music classes, as well as a weekly discussion group which

met to analyse books. Other classes sprang into existence periodically: for example, in chemistry, drawing, French, and mathematics.
There was a club which studied a method of phonetic shorthand
known as 'phonography' and a class in 'gymnastic and calisthenic
evolutions'. There were lectures on mesmerism, moral behaviour,
'Spectral Illusions', modern and ancient history, and many aspects
of science. W. J. Fox, the well-known Unitarian and anti-Corn
Law reformer, was a regular speaker at the Hall from 1846 on,
and many of his lectures were published subsequently. W. J.
Linton also lectured there frequently, as did Thomas Cooper on
politics, Dr John Epps on homeopathy and phrenology, William
Ellis on education, and a host of other speakers, some celebrated,
most little known except to those auto-didacts who zestfully
attended as many events as they could.

Lovett arranged for all of these activites. Some of the classes
were supervised directly by the trustees of the Hall; for these
free attendance was included in the general membership fee of
2d weekly, or 1d for female members. Other lectures were self-
financing, that is, registrants were required to pay a small fee
for admission. The sticking point was whether or not the lecturer
was willing to work for a low fee. Fox aided the NA immeasurably
by charging only a small sum for his appearances as a lecturer.
On the other hand, some orators volunteered their services gratis
in the hope that this would lead to a regular source of income.
Lovett negotiated with most of the class instructors and lecturers,
sometimes peremptorily refusing their services when he believed
them to be incompetent or insufficiently public-spirited. Once
he went to see Thomas Carlyle with an offer of five guineas per
lecture only to be informed that Carlyle was no longer giving
lectures.

The objective of the NA's myriad activities was to educate
and improve. The working classes had to be shown the path of
enlightenment. This was the key to rational change. Political

reform continued to be a primary objective for Lovett and his friends, but the belief took hold of them that it must be accompanied by educational and 'harmonious' activities. The development of the mind was best achieved through reading and analysis. Lovett loaned many of his own books to the NA and sold others to the organisation cheaply (including 'respectable' novels and collections of poetry); these formed the basis for its library of about 700 volumes. Other reformers contributed books and periodicals, including John Stuart Mill, who donated sets of the *London Review* and the *London and Westminster Review* to the NA, telling Lovett: 'I have never yet met with any associated body of men whom I respect so much as I do your association ...'.[3] Books were loaned to members for a small fee. The Sunday evening discussion classes were regarded as particularly important because these were the occasions for examining books and ideas carefully. Lovett or another member of the organisation would take the lead in interpreting a work; those present would then engage in vigorous discussion. Occasionally a participant would offer an original essay for analysis and debate.

Yet although intellectual development was the overriding preoccupation of the NA, its broad-based social and cultural events were considered equally important. 'Rational recreation' was assiduously cultivated. To compress the philosophy of these self-improving workingmen into something of a cliche, they conceived that a sound body was essential to a sound mind. Lovett and his associates distrusted the medical profession (though one does not find overt anti-medical feelings in NA tracts like that to be discovered in the writings of Carlile or Cobbett); instead they reposed confidence in a wholistic view of life in which strenuous 'moral' activity made both mind and body confident of itself. Individuals would then be able to combat evils foisted upon them by ignorance. Thus Lovett promoted tea parties, boat excursions, 'harmonic meetings', a Robert Burns Festival to celebrate the 'Spirit of Universal Brotherhood', and numerous other occasions when it was expected that good conversation would prevail in an atmosphere of rational intercourse.

At his initiative, the NA also sponsored musical evenings at which members played instrumental works for each other and sang songs that were intended to 'raise their minds above . . . drinking, fighting and degrading sentiments . . .'.[4] Lovett believed that music was ennobling; it reflected an 'irresistible' sense of human joy and had only to be purged of coarseness for it to work its magic on individuals. Dance was also 'spirit-stirring', with the further advantage that it strengthened the body's muscles. It had, however, to be decorous and respectable because of its sexual nature. This aspect of reformist culture has not yet been adequately studied. But it is important: in and for itself and as an index to byways of self-improvement which may help us to understand better both late nineteenth-century liberalism and the emergence of the labour movement.

The multifarious activities of the NA indicate how Lovett's thought was evolving from its earlier, more political tendencies. Yet, the organisation's 'silences' are also noteworthy. Although the minutes of the organisation hint at the suppressed hostility of members who were in disagreement over questions of substance, public controversy was kept to a minimum. Advocates of socialism, for example, were generally barred from the National Hall. There is a paradox here that requires some explanation. On the one hand, Lovett and others like him believed in the free exchange of ideas as the basis for social progress. At the same time, reflecting an optimism which had its roots in enlightenment thought, they considered the unity of mind of 'persons of all creeds and opinions' to be crucial. In theory the two points of view were resolvable; in practice, there were often differences of opinion, sometimes unforgiving ones. Lovett's religious views will be discussed subsequently, but it is important to note that he regarded theological controversy as an intellectual tool that weakened the working classes. At his urging, the NA prohibited any discussion of theology in its Hall, even in the weekly discussion classes. Likewise, alcohol was banned from the premises. Lovett believed that drink diminished rationality and was a source of social breakdown. The way to deal with this evil was to forbid it. Even in non-NA sponsored activities, when the Hall was leased to unaffiliated groups, a policy of temperance was rigorously enforced. Lovett met less resistance here than with religion (where Hetherington, Collet, and others opposed him). But some members grumbled. When in August 1843 he proposed that the NA undertake a public boycott of alcoholic beverages as a way to speed up reform he was defeated in the council. Likewise, the NA rejected his suggestion that it send a delegate to the World Temperance Convention in 1846.

Lovett was determined to establish an NA school for children and this proved a difficult task. In May 1843, a Sunday school was opened for the offspring of members and non-members. As many as 200 children attended the school initially, the only requirement being that they be 'clean in their person and clothing, and regular in their attendance'. There were five teachers in attendance, including Lovett and his wife. Reading, writing, and mathematics were taught, though not religion, which was the usual staple of Sunday school instruction. The school's goal was to give poor children – some of whom worked full-time – the opportunity to develop their rational faculties on what for many workingmen was considered a day of wasted resources. The Sunday school attracted favourable notice from reformers like William Ellis and George Combe, the phrenologist, whose book *The Constitution of Man* influenced Lovett's later development. But it was not successful. Within a short time, the number of pupils began to dwindle, making it difficult to pay teachers. Still, the Sunday school was conceived as an interim measure. The real expectation was that a day school might be established to complement the informal variety of adult education available at the Hall. Such a day school eventually materialised with the help of Ellis. But when it did it became in effect a substitute for the NA, which ceased to function shortly after the school's founding in 1848.

Lovett's resignation as secretary of the NA in November 1846 was provoked by an issue that had simmered for several years: theological controversy. It is well to consider the implications of this event because they bear upon his evolution as a reformer. Radical free thought was a significant aspect of working-class reform in the nineteenth century. It permeated Owenism and Chartism. Likewise, some of Lovett's closest allies were free thinkers, including Hetherington and Watson. Both men had been close to the wealthy atheist Julian Hibbert, who aided them financially until his death in 1834; from the early 1840s on, they supported George Jacob Holyoake, who had converted the radical deism of Paine into a 'liberal' version of free thought referred to as secularism. Free thought consisted of several strands: anti-clericalism, issues concerning the rights of Dissenters, the mooted disestablishment of the Church of England, and, most alarming to conservatives, direct attacks upon Christianity. In the early 1840s, several radical reformers, including Hetherington and Holyoake, were prosecuted for blasphemy.

Lovett's religious views are less clear than his educational and political commitments. Mark Hovell describes him as a secularist like Holyoake, while, ironically, Joseph McCabe, Holyoake's biographer, depicts him in censorious terms as a 'Christian Chartist'. More shrewdly, J. F. C. Harrison sees Lovett as influenced by 'general nonconformist Christianity'.[5] The truth is that, to some extent, he mixed together all of these views. During the most radical period of his life in the early 1830s, he was aggressively anti-clerical, sprinkling expressions like 'bloated Law-Church

Establishment' and 'people-devouring' clergy into his speeches and writings. The LWMA was not especially concerned with religion, but several times it too weighed in with unsparing attacks on the Church of England and clerical abuses in Ireland.

Political anti-clericalism remained part of Lovett's intellectual make-up for most of his life, and he continued to attack the traditional exploiting trinity of kings, priests, and aristocracy. But in the more controversial area of theology, he hedged his views. There is an ambiguity in his thought. For example, in the early 1840s he propounded a belief in 'enlightened inquiry', by which he meant a practical kind of deism in which morality was divorced from formal Christianity. Likewise, his educational proposals were entirely devoid of religious content. The NA strongly opposed the Education Bill of 1843 for fear it would lead to a school system dominated by religion. And in his autobiography, Lovett affirmed his non-credal views. When asked what his religion was at the time of his imprisonment in 1839, he recollects saying: 'I was of that religion which Christ taught, and which very few in authority practiced . . . but whether I was registered as Protestant, Catholic, or Infidel I know not'.[6]

Yet within the NA Lovett fought much harder against radical free thinkers than against those advocating a 'Christian Chartist' position. Two factions existed in the organisation and Lovett adhered to the more conservative group. Thus when the *National Association Gazette* condemned the Church of England for being 'corrupt and papistical' and called for the forcible appropriation of church funds to assist the poor, Lovett dissociated himself from the paper's views (while endorsing similar measures against the Church of Ireland). He did not side with those members of the NA who were exercised about the successful prosecution of Holyoake for blasphemy in 1842. And as mentioned previously, he was responsible for the exclusion of theological discussion from the National Hall.

In the summer of 1846 an organisational crisis erupted over the issue of theology. After the NA accepted an offer from Ellis to help establish a day school at the Hall, it appointed Lovett to be temporary superintendent. He was then approached by Holyoake, who was seeking a teaching position at the school with the encouragement of Place, a 'closet' free thinker. Whether intentionally or not, Lovett mishandled the offer. He did not reply to Holyoake, an unusual dereliction of courtesy from a man whose social skills were ordinarily impeccable. He then blamed Place for the ensuing confusion. The real explanation for Lovett's behaviour is to be found in his *Life and Struggles*, where he admits that he did not want Holyoake to teach at the school. The intrusion of 'Infidel' ideas by an 'avowed atheist' would, Lovett believed, destroy the school's non-sectarian character. Holyoake, a mild though contentious man, symbolised religious militancy to Lovett.

Within the council, Collet moved to censure Lovett, with the quiet backing of Hetherington and Watson. Lovett narrowly won the support of his colleagues, but not before much verbal blood was spilt. He then abruptly resigned as secretary, to be replaced by Charles Neesom after an interval of several months. With Lovett out as secretary (though still active in the organisation), the free thinkers briefly got the upper hand. In January 1847, the NA celebrated Thomas Paine's birthday for the first time, a festive occasion on many radical calendars. Then, as Lovett began to recover support within the association during 1847 and 1848, Hetherington and several other free thinkers defected from the NA to the newly founded John Street Institution, which offered a more congenial base for their activities.

Although the NA tried to extend its influence primarily by indirect means, at Lovett's urging it also adopted a series of straightforward political positions. It supported the Complete Suffrage Movement in 1842 and repeatedly attacked O'Connor's leadership of Chartism. (In turning down an invitation to be secretary of O'Connor's Land Association in 1843, Lovett described him as a 'physical-force blusterer'.) It issued statements endorsing Corn Law repeal and denouncing the physical intimidation of repealers by militant Chartists, on at least one occasion within the precincts of the National Hall. It condemned capital punishment and the Game Laws, endorsed reforms in Ireland, called for an end to factory abuses (though not repeal or even substantial reformation of the Poor Law), and reiterated with undiminished fervour its view that universal suffrage was the *sine qua non* of improvement since 'the right [to vote] belongs to every individual because he is a human being'.[7] In its political activities the NA also reflected two of Lovett's consuming interests: anti-slavery and internationalism.

Anti-slavery was the lesser of the two concerns but it does help to place Lovett's radical convictions in context. Slavery had been abolished in the British Empire by the 1840s; yet reformers like Lovett were concerned with its continuing existence in the United States. In part this reflected their romanticised image of America. For many workingmen in the nineteenth-century America was a 'beacon of freedom', a utopia of political and economic liberty at a time when oppression seemed to be more firmly ensconced than ever in Europe. In LWMA and NA propaganda there are wistful reminders of this perception. Yet the continuing existence of slavery in America cast a shadow across the dream.

Several historians have emphasised the interaction between the British and American anti-slavery campaigns. In the 1840s this link was strengthened. Abolitionists like William Lloyd Garrison and the ex-slave Frederick Douglass visited Britain, seeking to win the support of reformers. Lovett briefly became involved with this radical abolitionist phase of anti-slavery agitation when he joined the Anti-Slavery League, founded by the Garrisonians in 1846. Shortly afterwards he and Henry Vincent were elected to the council of the organisation. Lovett and Vincent believed that slavery was morally offensive and, in the former's eloquent words, was 'a link in the same great chain of oppression which binds the multitude in all countries and colonies'.[8] In 1846 Garrison lectured before a large crowd at the National Hall. He then solicited Lovett and Vincent to write a tract attacking slavery, which he proposed to circulate in the American abolitionist press. The invitation was not followed up after Garrison returned to America, leading to some slight unpleasantness between him and Lovett. But Lovett continued for many years to be involved in anti-slavery agitation.

More central was his internationalism, first evident in the pamphlets he wrote for the LWMA. Lovett has been described by Lewis Lorwin as 'the first working man of modern times with an international outlook'.[9] This is an exaggeration because the internationalist component of British radicalism stretched well back into the late eighteenth century. But Lovett stands foremost in the first half of the nineteenth century among radical reformers possessing such a vision. It was a central element of his career.

There is a schism in radical internationalism which Lovett's views reflect. On the one hand, he and other workingmen sympathised with continental nationalists, even to the extent of sometimes endorsing their revolutionary ambitions. Lovett knew and worked with leading emigrés in London, including Giuseppe Mazzini and the Polish exiles Stolzman and Worcell. He participated in agitation on their behalf and spent time with them socially. As a result, he frequently took a more aggressive line against foreign political oppression than his reputation as a moderate would indicate. Yet increasingly, he became persuaded of the need to make the world safe for rational reform by eliminating war and all sources of human conflict. In a sense, therefore, his thinking evolved from 'revolution' to peace, a progression traceable from the LWMA to the NA. But the two strands of his thought never quite coalesced.

Many publications of the LWMA, referred to previously, fused a sympathy for nationalism with class solidarity. This is clear, for example, in Lovett's *Address to the Working Classes of Belgium* (1836), a stirring plea on behalf of a workingman named Jacob Katz, and in subsequent addresses to Polish and French radicals. Lovett's basic demands – for a democratic suffrage, the right of work-ingmen to enjoy the full value of their produce, and popular education – were predicated on a vision of a world organised along lines of nationality. His outlook was Mazzinian at a time when Lovett had not yet read Mazzini, who moved to London in 1837.

Inexorably, Lovett began to mix revolutionary nationalism with peace. For a brotherhood to be established across national boundaries he believed it necessary to overthrow the 'selfish and despotic rulers of mankind'. Thus oppressed peoples everywhere (including the suffering poor in Britain) must remove the blinkers of ignorance from their eyes and create a 'holy alliance' of demo-cratic and moral feeling. Key words used by him made the point: enlightenment, fraternity, brotherhood, reason. In a series of LWMA tracts, he presented ideas that were both militant and pacifistic. But his goal was the same: to bring about a flood of reforms that would make Britain and other European countries repositories of democratic feeling.

The bifurcation in Lovett's thought became evident in the early 1840s, when he simultaneously attacked despotism and supported what one historian has referred to as 'pacificism' (meaning opposition to most wars under most circumstances). The minutes of the NA show Lovett taking the initiative on peace issues, as for example in the spring of 1843 when the organisation agreed to send an official representative to the World Peace Council, then meeting in London. Lovett maintained a steady fusillade of activity. This included the publication of addresses to reformers in the United States, France, and elsewhere on the subject of peace. In June 1844, he helped to convene a large public meeting at the National Hall to protest against the visit to Britain by Tsar Nicholas I, whom Lovett described as an 'active, wily tyrant; this chief personification of European despotism . . .'.[10] Nicholas embodied a retrograde image of Russia, while at the same time generating a powerful radical sympathy for Polish nationalism.

Italian nationalists also won support from Lovett, particularly because he and several other members of the NA were friendly with Mazzini, whose school for Italian boys was located on Greville Street opposite Lovett's lodgings. Lovett was involved in the famous 'Post Office Incident' in 1844. It was suspected at the time that Mazzini's mail was being opened by the Home Office in deference to Austria's influence with the government. This supposition proved correct. Linton, a close associate of the Italian nationalist, and Lovett combined to 'play a trick' on Sir James Graham, the Home Secretay, to determine if the accusation was valid. Lovett sent a letter to Mazzini which, it was subsequently demonstrated, had been opened before it reached him. The incident became a *cause célèbre* when Thomas Duncombe raised the matter in the House of Commons. As a result, the practice of keeping emigré nationalists under tight surveillance by reading their mail was stopped for a time.

In 1844, Lovett helped to organise the Democratic Friends of all Nations, a Mazzinian association. Linton was also active in this group, which included Prussian, Italian, and Polish refugees together with British middle-class and working-class radicals. It was the first of several international associations based in London which espoused the cause of continental nationalism in the 1840s, although it is less well known than the more radical Fraternal Democrats, founded in 1845, to which Marx and Engels had ties.

Lovett persuaded the NA to fund half of the expenses of the Democratic Friends of all Nations and drafted its *Address to the Friends of Humanity and Justice* (1845), setting forth its objectives. He attacked the 'almost universal reign of oppression and injustice throughout the world', as well as the widespread existence of 'selfishness, force and fraud' and 'exclusive political power'.[11] His proffered solution was for the poor to take non-violent steps to rectify these evils, notably increased moral solidarity and better education. This moderate line clearly was not the answer for many continental radicals, and it led to Lovett's resignation from the organisation, although he continued to support it privately. At the same time, he strongly attacked the views of the Fraternal Democrats, led by Harney, who implied that nationalism was an intermediate step on the path to international revolution. In April 1847, Lovett helped to found the more moderate People's International League, a Mazzinian organisation headed by Linton and Thomas Cooper, which, however, emphasised national self-determination at the expense of peace. Some of Lovett's closest allies, including Richard Moore and John Parry, were active in the PIL. But he soon left it in the belief that it also was too extreme.

By the mid-1840s peace had become a primary goal for Lovett as he drifted further away from mainstream working-class radicalism and attempted to take shelter in a reformist vision more acceptable to Nonconformists and liberals. Among the leading anti-war activists of the period were Sturge and Miall, Lovett's erstwhile colleagues in the Complete Suffrage Movement, together with Richard Cobden and John Bright, the leading exponents of free trade. Peace and free trade merged together in the mid-1840s. For many reformers the former could best be achieved when all barriers to the exchange of goods and ideas were torn down. Freedom from external pressures, whether economic or military, was regarded as the way to create a world safe from the scourge of war. War meant wastefulness of goods and men. It implied an irrationality that contradicted natural principles of justice. Lovett and his associates believed it self-evident that a world free from external barriers was desirable; this could best be accomplished if people did not allow themselves to be bullied into the use of military force, which was invariably employed for narrow ends.

Within the NA Lovett repeatedly took the view that the working classes were the chief victims of war. In his *Address to the Working Classes of France* (1844) he described military conflict as a crime against poor people and 'the most formidable impediment to the civilisation of the race'. The alternatives were stark: the unfolding of moral and civil greatness or 'a holocaust of life and wealth'.[12] In other NA publications he reaffirmed this manichaean view. On one side of an imaginary line were 'savage demons, thirsting for blood' who constantly placed in danger the 'improvement towards a higher state of civilisation and happiness'[13]; on the other was an educated working class which, when united with the middle classes, would achieve a 'COMING OF AGE OF FREEDOM, PEACE, AND BROTHERHOOD'.[14] There was a powerful element of idealism in Lovett's thought which mid-Victorian peace societies sometimes expressed. For him, however, this idealism was not religious, as it was for Sturge and Miall; nor was it primarily economic, as it was for Cobden. Rather, it exemplified a type of moral illuminism shorn of political trappings. Lovett was optimistic about the chances for peace, almost as if the decline of his political influence had given him an incentive to reach out for the future.

In the 1840s the Peel Government attempted to revive the system of militia drawings which had been halted since Lovett's campaign in 1831. This retrograde step was condemned by reformers and the NA convoked several public meetings on the subject. Arguments similar to those of 1831 were deployed. Using the vocabulary of pacifism, Lovett came close to reformulating his earlier view: that the people must not co-operate with militarism even if this meant refusing to obey the law. Yet essentially, he stuck to more moderate views: condemnations of the 'war spirit', invidious comparisons between adult combat and children's war games (all traces of the latter were banned from NA schools), attacks upon the meretricious values of heroism and bravery, and the reiterated assertion (as in his *Humble Apology for Peace*, 1844) that war is 'the antagonist of morality, religion, science, literature and art, and all that refine and elevate humanity.'[15] He also backed specific proposals for ending wars, such as Cobden's call for an international body to arbitrate disputes between nations.

In the final analysis, Lovett, torn between his sympathies for nationalism and peace, put on the armour of enlightenment to repel reaction. Political, educational, economic, even moral issues could be resolved, he believed, if intellect were enabled to gain superiority over brute force. 'All history and experience testify that mind is a greater conqueror than strength', he maintained.[16] This had not yet happened, and given Lovett's weak institutional base, there was little reason to think it would happen in the immediate future. Abstract commitment offers a degree of consolation when practical solutions fall short, however, and Lovett, increasingly a prophet of education, found himself to an extent relying on a psychological crutch.

When he ceased to be secretary of the NA in November 1846, Lovett lost his only regular source of income. Fortunately, the Quaker publisher William Howitt came to his aid at about this time. Howitt had come to know Lovett as a participant in anti-slavery and peace meetings. His attitude towards workingmen was like that of Sturge and other Complete Suffrage advocates. In March 1846 he became part proprietor of the weekly *People's Journal*, which had been founded by John Saunders several months previously. The paper backed many causes advocated by Lovett, including temperance, education, and the formation of work-ingmen's mutual improvement societies. As a favour to Lovett, who needed the income, Howitt made him publisher of the journal in the summer of 1846, at a time when his position in the NA was under attack from the supporters of Holyoake. Lovett's name never actually appeared on the paper (John Bennett was listed as publisher). But he did accept the job, and in late 1846 and early 1847 the paper began to print miscellaneous NA material, including accounts of some of its activities. Then, some time in 1847, Lovett's connection with the *People's Journal* ended. Howitt quarrelled with Saunders and left in February; Lovett probably departed shortly afterwards. Howitt then funded the better-known *Howitt's Journal* with his wife Mary but there is no evidence that Lovett was connected with it during the two years of its existence.

In 1848, when Chartist demonstrations took place in London and elsewhere leading to the presentation of the third National Petition in April, Lovett became involved once again in the efforts to gain the People's Charter. His opinions about the sources of political evil had not changed since the early 1840s. He still believed that Whig and Tory factions were chiefly responsible for economic and political abuses. According to Lovett, writing in 1848 but sounding very much like the reformer of a decade earlier, by 'their laws, their monopolies, their rules, had England been pauperised and her people enslaved'.[17] The only new factor in the situation was the emergence of liberal middle-class refor-mers who were now asserting themselves because they had achieved some of their own ends, including Corn Law repeal. Lovett was adamant that the working classes must not rely upon the middle classes for leadership. Activism could not be stimulated externally; the people had to 'learn to think and act for them-selves, they must build up their own liberties or they will never be truly free.' Yet, somewhat inconsistently, he pushed hard for an alliance with the middle classes, believing that 'the wise and good of all classes' must unite against a privileged minority who were 'maintaining the monopolies, perpetuating their unjust powers, and taxing our population'.[18]

Lovett would have nothing to do with mainstream Chartism which, he believed, still typified 'violence and folly'. He deplored what he perceived as class hatreds being disseminated by O'Connor and other Chartist leaders, and repudiated the 'blundering' monster demonstration of 10 April on Kennington Common. He shunned the brief Chartist National Assembly of May 1848 (as did O'Connor) on the ground that it was an illegal body. But his personal commitment to the People's Charter and to a vision of reform based upon a detestation of corruption and social inequality remained little changed.

During the late 1840s, there were several attempts to bring about an alliance between middle-class and working-class reformers. Among those seeking closer ties were Sturge and Miall of the old Complete Suffrage party, Cobden and Joseph Hume among the parliamentary reformers, Bronterre O'Brien who was now advocating land and currency reform as a way to resolve social questions, and moderate working-class reformers (in addition to Lovett) like Thomas Cooper, Hetherington, and Linton. Lovett rejected O'Brien's schemes because they seemed to him to possess little of political value. But he tried to accommodate those parliamentary and middle-class reformers who favoured a compromise based on a variation of household suffrage. Lovett would not accept the substance of their demands. He was still wedded to the integrity of the Charter with its Six Points. He continued to believe that the principle of justice would not allow the moral worth of individuals to be reduced to a mere 'money qualification'. Yet, he was prepared to concede some of the symbolism of the Charter, a significant shift from 1842. Thus he agreed that the phrasing of the document might be altered, so long as any adjustments were minor.

A group calling itself the National Alliance was formed in 1846 to support the extension of the franchise by 'just, peaceful, legal, and constitutional means'. This formula was similar to that of the Complete Suffrage Union in 1842, and the organisation attracted a wide phalanx of supporters, from Vincent and Parry of the NA to Sturge and W. J. Fox, middle-class reformers whom Lovett respected. Lovett wrote *An Address to the Radical Reformers of the United Kingdom* on behalf of this group. He attempted to broaden their base, by making clear the need for a universal suffrage commitment if the House of Commons was to be transformed into a 'true representation of the wants and wishes of the whole people'.[19] In his appeal he compassed middle-class reforms like free trade (no longer as emotional an issue as it had been), a reduction of national expenditure, and a tax on property.

In May 1848, the People's League was founded. Lovett, Lowery, Vincent, and Miall were members, though not Hume or Cobden. (A more radical rival organisation, the People's Charter Union, headed by Thomas Cooper, included Hetherington, Holyoake, and Watson among its members.) Lovett was appointed secretary of the People's League and composed several of its addresses, in which he voiced his commitment to radical reform, while emphasising the non-violent philosophy of the organisation's sponsors. Among other things he called for 'Score Petitions', carrying twenty signatures each, which were to record support for universal suffrage, 'the only radical cure for those political corruptions and social burthens which exclusive legislation has generated and which our aristocratic rulers seemed resolved to maintain'.[20]

The People's League wilted for lack of support, in part because of Lovett's unwillingness to compromise on political democracy. In *Justice Safer than Expediency*, a pamphlet he wrote in 1848, he refused to accept household suffrage or a lodger franchise, an improved variation of it. On the other hand, Hume and Cobden, the most influential proponents of what came to be known as the 'Little Charter' (which, curiously, was supported by O'Connor), favoured household suffrage and financial reform. Lovett hoped that the People's League would 'grow in numbers and improve in principle', and that the two MPs might be 'induced to join'. He did not know Hume particularly well nor did he repose much confidence in Place, who was working behind the scenes on behalf of the People's League. But as secretary of the organisation, Lovett tried to use his reputation for integrity to promote the cause of universal suffrage. It was insufficient. The pincers of middle-class pusillanimity and Chartist antagonism closed in on him once again, for the last time politically as it turned out. He refused to support a middle-class-sponsored National Parliamentary and Financial Reform Association, established in 1849, and played no further role in the movement for political reform.

What were the prospects for the kind of reforms Lovett hoped to see carried out? After the failures of 1848-49, these seemed to him to rest exclusively on educational and moral improvement, an analysis endorsed by other workingmen who were disillusioned at this time with the political failures of the 1840s and began to seek 'non-political' remedies for their grievances. As Lovett foresaw, this individualistic approach was unlikely to yield concrete political results in the near future. Still, it offered significant possibilities for self-improvement and personal respectability. This was no small consolation for him. Fortified by a fresh dose of conviction in the form of a 'conversion' to political economy in 1847, he prepared himself for the third and final phase of his career.

7 A spirit misplaced

Francis Place has described Lovett as a 'spirit misplaced', and the words seem appropriate to the final 28 years of his life. After 1848 he cut his ties with institutional politics. He maintained contacts with only a few of the working-class radicals with whom he had been friendly in previous years, making friendships instead with political economists like William Ellis. Lovett became an advocate of liberal individualism. At times, he adhered to an extreme form of moral self-discipline and bore witness to it in his activities. He was 'dogged' and 'disillusioned', in the words of G. D. H. Cole, traits that while not entirely overshadowing his general optimism, seem to distort the balance of this final phase of his life.

In his early years as an agitator, Lovett had worked effectively in the mainstream of popular radicalism. In the early 1840s he had moderated his views and begun to favour education as a substitute for politics. From 1847 on, convinced that moral reform held the exclusive key to progress, he preached, so to speak, against the political odds. Some of his positions reflected a developing liberal consensus, others a personal crotchetiness. By moving decisively from 'left' to 'right' within a decade, Lovett seemed to prompt legitimate questions about the relationship between artisan politics and the radical and liberal traditions. Where was he going from this point on? How did he propose to get there? Was there anything inevitable about this progression?

At the outset of this final phase of his life, Lovett was fêted handsomely for his services to the cause of reform. He had increased his reputation among his supporters by being elected a few years before to the vestry of the parish of St Pancras and as a Poor Law Guardian. But his financial situation continued to be parlous and his friends, with Parry presiding, held a testimonial dinner in his honour in February 1848. He was presented with a gift of 140 sovereigns offered in a tricolour purse. The symbolism was apposite to the occasion. For it revived some of the reformist buoyancy of the past. Moderate Chartists like Vincent and Cooper appeared at the National Hall to reaffirm their belief that Lovett, the man who had started the Chartist movement back in 1837, continued to represent its best political tendencies.

An address composed by W. J. Fox helped to feed the myth that was already beginning to envelop Lovett. He was described as an unbending advocate of reason and peace, and in personal terms as a model of 'integrity, purity, firmness, zeal, and benevolence'. Lovett responded in kind. He admitted to some political misdeeds (though always in the cause of unity). But he reiterated his faith in mental emancipation and, in a phrase reflecting the beliefs of his final years, paid homage to 'individual and national morality'. It was one of those moving occasions that are a quintessential part of the social texture of popular radicalism. The pathos was enhanced by its finality. For it was the last time Lovett's virtues were to be publicly celebrated during his lifetime. Henceforth he was to be limited to quiet paths of progress.

Before considering the extensive transformation in Lovett's thought in 1847, it is important to focus once more on his work as an educator. Education was the leading practical motif of his last years. It gave substance to his activities, helping to counteract the decline of his political influence. In February 1848 two day schools were established by the NA with money donated by William Ellis, a political economist and educator. These schools had been in the process of formation for almost two years and were central to Lovett's educational efforts. When the NA folded in 1849 he was made manager of the National Hall (which continued to sponsor lectures) and supervisor of these schools, where he also taught. He served in this dual capacity until 1857, when both the schools and the Hall were wound up after a dispute with the landlord of the property, who converted the premises into a music-hall. It was an unfitting anti-climax for Lovett: one of his best efforts at improvement had given way (in his own words) to 'an institution for corrupting the rising generation'.[1] Yet during the years 1848-57 he ran the schools successfully. He became a fully-fledged disciple of Ellis, who supported him financially for several years. He conducted the schools along lines suggested by Ellis, whose credentials as an educator dated from 1848, when he commenced the first of a number of day schools for poor children in different parts of London which were known as Birkbeck schools.

About 300 children attended the two NA schools between 1848 and 1857. Many were part-time pupils; others left after a few months to work full-time or because their parents could not afford to pay the low fees required. Difficulties like these were customary in working-class schools of the time and Lovett, who continued to be in poor physical health, coped with them as well as expected. He did much of the teaching in both schools himself, borrowing pedagogical techniques from the Birkbeck schools, ten of which were established in the 1850s. Lovett also theorised about education, based particularly on his readings of Pestalozzi, the eighteenth-century Swiss educationalist. The crucial thing, according to Lovett, was to make education fit into a total pattern of life skills. It had to be as practical as possible, so that it could be used effectively outside the classroom. At the same time, it must be enjoyable. To this end, he devised a method of teaching spelling by cards as a 'game and amusement', much like modern spelling bees. Lovett considered ideas less important than 'reality' and he down-played books (partly in deference to a scarcity of funds). His pupils were introduced to 'objects' and taught skills, the most important of which was the ability to relate what they learned to social and political reformation. Lovett's message was clear: a resolution of life's tribulations was dependent upon knowledge. To make sense out of what was being taught, one had to focus on the need for improvement.

Some of Lovett's educational nostrums are interesting, others little more than a precis of the 'progressive' educational jargon of the time. But he attempted to apply his ideas with something like his old zest. When George Combe, the author of the *Constitution of Man*, an influential work on phrenology, visited the schools, he commended them highly. Combe observed Ellis giving some lectures on social economy, which he liked; he also singled out for praise Lovett's science class, an integral part of the curriculum. Lovett believed that science (he defined it broadly to include moral and political as well as physical science) held the key to human development. It was essential to every aspect of life. It encompassed the resources necessary to the advancement of knowledge. And if taught properly – he had alluded frequently to this point in his pamphlets of the 1830s and 1840s – it would arouse the 'latent genius' in poor people, enabling them to overcome the present 'incrustation of ignorance, prejudice, and vice'.[2]

This belief in the efficacy of scientific knowledge was a chief ingredient in popular reform during the middle decades of the century. However, Lovett not only employed the rhetoric of an improving science to advance his educational claims; he sought to do something practical to disseminate it. Finding that proper teaching materials were not available, he wrote several scientific textbooks. Two of them remained unpublished although they were used in his own schools as well as in several other schools. They dealt with astronomy and geology, which he regarded as of particular importance because they demonstrated the 'limitless' possibilities of human endeavour. A third textbook – on zoology

– was never completed. It was more ambitious than the others, however, because it was intended not only for use in the classroom but as a way of circulating knowledge among workingmen.

Lovett's *Elementary Anatomy and Physiology*, an illustrated textbook which he published in 1851, was a phenomenon of sorts. The subject speaks for itself. It was controversial, even daring: in fact, Lovett was one of the first British educators to teach anatomy to elementary school pupils. He did it in his own schools and in several of the Birkbeck schools. Classrooms were segregated by sex, a necessary undertaking if respectability was to be maintained. Yet, based upon a reading of the textbook, the lessons must have been unusually explicit. Large anatomical drawings from the book were mounted on strips of calico in the classroom. The children were seated in semicircles and drilled on what they saw. Lovett's objective was to stimulate a dialectical process: regurgitation as a means of understanding. What makes *Elementary Anatomy and Physiology* so interesting (in addition to its specificity) were the moral lessons it was intended to convey. It inculcated wholism: a linkage of morality and physical health. Lovett tacked on to his descriptive and mostly derivative chapters on the human body sections dealing with temperance, diet, and exercise. He made the point repeatedly that 'excess' was likely to produce a physically deranged and warped person: a combination of mental illness and social crime. Thus as well as being a pedagogical aid, *Elementary Anatomy and Physiology* was a plea for self-improvement: 'the temple of our moral nature, the seat of the ennobling virtues in the extended brotherhood of man'.[3]

Like Ellis, Lovett was insistent about the secular nature of his schools. Sectarian Christian teaching was banned, which made them almost unique among the schools of the time. In Lovett's opinion, Christian teaching was responsible for obstructing the spread of knowledge because '*bigotry* under the name of *religion*' had stultified 'the great effort of making education the instrument of *mental freedom* and *national progress*'.[4] Morality must be the basic component of teaching: a morality divorced from the preachments of organised religion. In this sense, Lovett's 'practical' Christian beliefs remained in the forefront of his thought. He intended his schools to teach duties and responsibilities, enabling the children attending them to become 'wise, good, and useful members of society'. Even so, some reformers were reluctant to endorse Lovett's approach to education. Richard Moore, for example, who held no brief for organised religion and was Lovett's friend, expressed concern that the schools might try to inculcate partisan ideas. There is no tangible evidence that this happened except in the generalised sense of trying to instill a concept of good citizenship.

Lovett was a solid educator. His agenda was confined to doing and thinking; the rest, he believed, would follow without any need for prodding. During these years, his opinions about the role of government in education continued to evolve. In *Chartism* he had proposed that education be privately subscribed (although his 1837 tract on education had accepted a financial role for government). The advantage of private education was that those benefiting from it would be encouraged to make additional efforts. However, Lovett realised how difficult it was to put this ideal into practice, and he became receptive once more to demands for governmental involvement. In his book *Social and Political Morality*, which he published in 1853, he urged that schools be funded through rates and controlled by district committees appointed by ratepayers. It was essential that these committees be responsive to the needs of the students; otherwise, even in this hybrid structure with its emphasis on local initiative, the groundwork would be laid for a 'state moulding power, which no government should possess'.[5]

Lovett spent a substantial portion of the last twenty-eight years of his life teaching children. Apart from Ellis's continuing largesse, this provided him with his sole source of income. After the collapse of the National Hall in 1857, he taught for ten more years: at the St Thomas Charterhouse Schools in London, which were under Unitarian control, and at a small grammar school in Gray's Inn Road. Ellis recommended him to both positions, becoming in effect his patron as well as his benefactor. Although Lovett's bronchial and intestinal disabilities worsened during these years, and he found teaching to be more demanding physically than anything he had done previously, he enjoyed his new profession and, by all odds, became quite adept at it.

Still, Lovett is far better known as the man who educated adults, whose activities prefigure the Working Men's College movement of the 1860s and the establishment of the Workers' Educational Association in 1905. Mostly his reputation in adult education rests upon activities interspersed throughout many years, including his work in the LWMA and the NA and as an inspirer of educational self-help. For many years, Lovett urged that recreational facilities be built in pleasant surroundings, away from the lure of public houses and taverns. In 1829, he drafted a petition for the opening of museums and libraries on Sundays. In this petition, which gained several thousand signatures, he emphasised the importance of 'useful knowledge' and 'rational instruction and amusement', particularly on the only day of leisure available to workingmen. Lovett contended that there should be encouragement for 'instructive lectures to be given to the mass of the people' on Sundays.[6]

Although this petition received little support in the Commons, Lovett returned countless times to the theme of the diffusion of knowledge. It forms the core of *Chartism* and of the testimony he gave to the Select Committee on Public Libraries in 1849. On the latter occasion he urged forcefully that circulating libraries for adult workingmen should be created. Such libraries, in his opinion, were best managed by their readers, perhaps through annual elections. Likewise, he favoured coffeehouses for musical and other 'rational' forms of recreation. As a member of the Working Class Committee on the Great Exhibition of 1851, Lovett encouraged workingmen to visit the Crystal Palace exhibits in Hyde Park, with their magnificent demonstrations of industrial progress. It is an exaggeration to describe Lovett's contribution to adult education in unstinted terms because the only pedagogical institutions he established were the informal models in the LWMA and the NA. But in his understated way he heralded future advances in this area. At the least, he modelled his own life upon the ideal of the self-improving artisan who had come to recognise the transcendent importance of mind.

Temperance was an integral facet of Lovett's commitment to education and moral improvement. He was by no means alone in this. Vincent, Lowery, Hetherington, and Watson among his closest associates were all active temperance reformers. Respectability, so potent an element of artisan culture, depended for its success upon temperance. The latter was linked to education because it presupposed a prudential approach to life. By abstaining from alcoholic beverages, a workingman was thought to be able to harness his energy and skills to a future that relied upon conservation of effort. The alternative was frivolity and waste. And in the mid-Victorian decades frivolity implied 'irrational' amusements like gambling, 'low' songs in music-halls, keeping late hours, being sexually immoral, and failing to work hard. Lovett and his colleagues, by constantly emphasising the need for mental effort and self-discipline, sought to avert such a breakdown.

Although he belonged to the United Kingdom Alliance from its founding in 1853, Lovett was not notably involved in the organised temperance campaign, which was in the mainstream of the reform movement. Instead he made his point quietly in 'educational' ways. In the 1830s, he published several essays in the unstamped press setting out the case for temperance. His LWMA tracts and *Chartism* include dire warnings about the evils of the 'soul-degrading vice of drink', which he believed was prevalent among 'the most ignorant of the working classes'. Lovett would not allow the LWMA to hold any of its meetings in public houses (a departure from the common radical practice), and at his insistence the NA adopted a policy of strict temperance in 1844. To his personal credit, he was not fanatical about his own habits. Occasionally Lovett had a glass of wine at social or political functions, though never beer or spirits; he claimed to be 'mentally and bodily better for it'.[7] He reminded readers of his *Life and Struggles* that he had taught himself to do right. As a young cabinet-maker without a proper certificate, he had been under pressure to win over his workmates by treating them (a practice known as 'footings'). He had generally refused to participate, and had believed this to be a turning point in his life because it demonstrated the virtue of personal fortitude.

Lovett felt that economic misgovernment created the conditions in which intemperance prevailed. Thus as part of his own Owenite credo in the 1830s, he advocated a non-competitive system of production and distribution to eliminate the long hours of work and poor conditions which were an incentive to drink. As late as 1840, in *Chartism*, he proffered the claim that the most efficacious remedy for intemperance was a 'just government'. Yet as he became convinced of the need for more education, he switched tactics. Change must come from within, he averred, opting for the 'moral suasionist' side of the temperance argument. And he became increasingly confident that it would. He told the Select Committee on Libraries that public behaviour was improving because of the spread of reading. The use of alcohol had declined noticeably, as had brutality and coarse language. Economic and political advantages were likely to result, including a productive labour force and the diminution of squalor, crime, and pauperism, 'the far greater portion of which is due to drunkenness and drinking habits'.

Twenty years later, writing as 'An Old Reformer' in the *Alliance News* (the organ of the United Kingdom Alliance), Lovett was more pessimistic. Drink, he reported, was still the 'demoralising curse of our country'. It continued to encourage 'low slang' . . . inane songs, and the all-absorbing love of dress, pleasure and amusement'.[8] He observed that 'the best efforts of the sober and intelligent part [of the people] are still marred by the drunken and the dissolute'.[9] Given the failure of propaganda, it is not surprising that Lovett now supported the efforts of the prohibitionists. Accordingly, he favoured the UKA proposal to prohibit off-licences from selling wine and spirits. And he endorsed the Permissive Bill of 1870, which empowered the majority of residents in a district to ban spirits altogether. So strongly did Lovett feel about this idea (which was not accepted by Parliament) that he accepted the proposal of some prohibitionists that brewers and publicans not be compensated for their losses. Why not give the money to unemployed workers instead? he asked. There were rhetorical echoes of his earlier days in these words.

Lovett's commitment to education and temperance – complementary enthusiasms which span many incidents in his life – must not deflect us from considering the dramatic shift in his thought which occurred beginning in 1847. This 'conversion' marks the third and final phase of his career. The failure of historians to demarcate it from Lovett's previous activities has led to confusion about where he stood. Until at least the mid-1840s, Lovett's vision of economic and political change continued to be basically that of a skilled artisan. His sympathy with the claims of the working classes was articulated in the framework of the old radical tradition of 'us' versus 'them'. Lovett felt aggrieved at the injustices suffered by the poor: the heavy burden of taxation, the privileges exercised by landlords and newly emergent capitalists, the weight of an oppressive state church, above all a political system which barred from participation all those who did not meet the requirements of property. His vision, shared by many Chartists, was that of the small producer. He wanted honest labour to be recognised and rewarded. This meant real productivity and an end to speculation and the spiralling of debts. His class feelings were tempered yet solid: for example, in 1841 he praised William Cobbett as 'ever the consistent advocate of the sons of labour ... [because] he strove incessantly during a long life, to remove every obstacle, political and social, which marred the happiness of the labourer's home'.[10]

In the aftermath of the breakdown of the first Complete Suffrage conference in the spring of 1842, the *National Association Gazette* summarised Lovett's outlook when it affirmed its belief in 'a system, in which every man able and willing to work, shall earn the means of existence. [Such workers] want no laws to raise their labour to an artificial value; they rather want the abolition of those laws which depress their labour below its fair and natural value'.[11] Lovett's emphasis on moral force and education in the early 1840s represented a shift in his thinking. He made it absolutely clear that he would have no truck with militant rhetoric or action. All of his energy was to be directed to self-improvement. But though politically marginalised, the NA still functioned within a tradition of working-class self-help and class-consciousness. Lovett continued for the next few years to reject the ideas of middle-class reformers like Miall, Sturge, and Place whenever these clashed with his own beliefs. As late as the beginning of 1847, in *A Proposal for the Consideration of the Friends of Progress*, a 1d tract published by John Cleave, Lovett restated many of his customary beliefs while calling for a 'General Association of Progress'.

Then, in 1847, against the backdrop of the theological frictions within the NA, a break occurred. It accentuated Lovett's partiality to 'respectability' and stripped him of the last vestiges of a class outlook. It made him almost a caricature of his former self as he articulated theories of political economy which were lifted straight from the pages of William Ellis and John Stuart Mill in particular. Parts of this vision were radical. But it bore little relation to the Lovett of earlier years in its pronounced individualism and abandonment of universal suffrage. The 'Old Reformer' who wrote anonymously in the pages of the *Bee-Hive* in the late 1860s was like a veteran jockey who emerges to ride one more race. He knows that some of his skills are gone and that only the memory of what he had once achieved is still there. To a very considerable extent, the 'moral force' Lovett of Hovell and the educational Lovett of Tawney (who are best known to students) are not this later veteran jockey, but the transitional figure of the 1840s.

Ellis's influence on Lovett has not been given due weight by other historians but it was decisive. Ellis initially financed the schools Lovett managed at the National Hall, subsidised him privately for many years, and converted him to political economy. His book *Outlines of Social Economy*, written in 1846, had a considerable influence on many workingmen. It contains 'lessons' on taxation, money, the laws of supply and demand, labour, and related political and social issues. Ellis was himself a recent convert to political economy, but from 1846 on he was a vigorous propagandist for the cause. His views attracted Lovett because they down-played theory in favour of practical stratagems. Education was the primary means to social advancement for Ellis as he attempted to weld the concrete and the general into a total view of life.

Lovett's *Social and Political Morality*, written over a period of several years and published in 1853, is a paraphrase of the ideas of Ellis, to whom it is dedicated. Lovett's major theme, prefigured in the work of the NA, is that 'the liberty, prosperity, and happiness of our country have their foundation in the morals of the people'. Extremes must be avoided if a good life, socially and individually, is to be achieved. The emphasis is on those virtues subsequently labelled 'Victorian': thrift, hard work, the accumulation of knowledge, temperance, the promotion of the 'civilisation and brotherhood of man'.[12] Many of the pages of *Social and Political Morality* read like a simple textbook on ethics. Criminals are deemed guilty of 'moral imperfections', which they are likely to pass on to their children; drunkenness represents a failed aspiration because it allows 'political tricksters [to] bribe their way to power'; stealing is a gross evil when 'so much of the general prosperity and happiness of a country depends upon the security of property'.[13] According to Lovett, economy and frugality are 'the great moving powers ... that gradually build up those productive powers, which render nations prosperous and free'. To be sure, many lives have been ruined by economic exploitation and rapaciousness. But the only truly inferior people, he insists, are 'those whose own vices have degraded them'.[14]

Social and Political Morality also expounds Lovett's political commitments: to universal suffrage (not yet abandoned), free trade, the settlement of international disputes, and the need (ambiguously phrased) to improve 'social welfare'. There is also a passage in which he condemns employers who treat their workers as a 'mere human mechanism'. Here he seems fleetingly to be reverting to the Lovett of twenty years before who expressed indignation at the brutalities of the new industrial system. But instantly, like the political economists whom he now followed, Lovett affirms that legislation is not the solution to economic injustice. The latter is to be found in self-knowledge, understanding, and the proper application of wealth. Charity (or artificial political interference) will only encourage an 'idle, dissolute, and vicious life'.

Lovett advocated a number of changes in *Social and Political*

Morality which indicate how far he had travelled from the early 1840s. He cites Mill in arguing for a land tax and an inheritance tax on land because (in old radical terms) the '*absolute right* to the land of the country belong to the people'. He endorses legal and prison reforms reflecting the influence of Bentham. He maintains that the majority of crimes are committed by '*untrained or ill-trained classes*':[15] for this reason, it is desirable to reclaim offenders through a training programme, including prison farms where convicts can measure their improvement by earning some money. Although still in favour of allowing trade unions to organise, Lovett now seems to accept the Ricardian idea that they are useless appendages which at best can instil in workers a sense of pride as they struggle for better conditions. Lovett also advocates a lessening in the competition for jobs, and the emigration of workers, though not the Malthusian nostrum of population control. In the 1860s he began to favour this as well.

There are traces of both the 'early' and the 'middle' Lovett in *Social and Political Morality*. But mostly it is Lovett the political economist and exponent of Victorian liberalism who is on view. This is most clearly expressed in his statements about women. Lovett has been hailed as a pioneer advocate of women's rights. In some ways, he was. For example, the petition of February 1837, which he wrote and which was in effect the first draft of the People's Charter, stipulated that women should be entitled to vote. Lovett was committed to *universal* political rights at a time when most radical reformers were not. Both the LWMA and particularly the NA sought to give women a measure of equality. In so doing, they emulated those Owenite associations which integrated women into their social programmes, whereas Chartist groups like the NCAs preferred to organise women as political auxiliaries. Most of the female members of the NA were spouses and daughters of male members, but nonetheless they were admitted by a formal process of nomination and election.

They participated in the activities of the NA, sometimes in separate classes and usually at reduced prices. The *NA Gazette* strongly advocated the 'equal educational, social, and political rights of woman as well as man', while attacking the 'conventional propriety' which restrained women's behaviour. According to the paper, propriety 'cramped [a woman's] faculties, and limited her aspirations'.[16]

During the second or NA phase of his career, Lovett became more conventional in his attitudes towards women. For example, he made much of the need to educate them, including his own wife and daughter Kezia, who later became an actress. However, the reason was not intellectual equality for its own sake. He believed that if the moral and intellectual abilities of women were developed they would be able to train properly the males under them. Their sons would grow up to be model reformers. In a poem 'Woman's Mission', published in 1856 but written about fourteen years earlier, Lovett rhapsodised in true early Victorian style about the mission of women:[17]

> How much depends on woman's care and love,
> Whether man soars to excellence and use,
> His country to improve, his race to bless;
> Or sinks in vice, a stunted blighted trunk . . . .

Women therefore were to be treated as equals in order to speed up the collapse of 'oppression, misery, ignorance, and wrong'.[18]

This is conventional thinking but it is advanced (some female reformers made the same point as a way of selling their political arguments to a sceptical public). Mixed in with it is the notion of a separate sphere for women *and* that women were unduly restricted. They were, observed Lovett, 'claimed as man's property, his pet, or slave. . .'.[19] Anticipating John Stuart Mill's later arguments, he asserted that it was in a man's interest to have a free woman as a partner and spouse.

He, like all despots pleased with power, will hold
And firmly grasp, and think his bonds secure. . . .

More striking – and seemingly derived from Owenite sources –
was Lovett's suggestion that the institution of marriage might
be oppressive whenever a good woman found herself tied by
'chains of holy church' to a 'dotard, drunkard, gambler, knave or
beast'. Divorce was the way to sever such a connection but Lovett
knew that only the rich could 'break such legal bonds', at least
before the Marriage Act of 1857.

By comparison with the complex and interesting Lovett of
the 1840s, Lovett the political economist was irredeemably conventional in his treatment of women. Although he was wedded
to sexual equality in principle, there was a marked shift in
his pronouncements on the subject. He now justified a double
standard in the name of self-improvement. In the pages of *Social
and Political Morality*, he characterised unchastity as a 'polluting
vice' which, more than any other, contributed to 'the deterioration and destruction of mental and bodily health'.[20] Women
were abjured to behave prudently both before and after marriage:
to be clean and respectable at all times. They had to be 'wives
and mothers in demeanour, . . . earnest and helpful in all that
concerns their family or their country'.[21] Admittedly some women
were paying the price of exploitation in the form of prostitution
and social breakdown ('lascivious romance and painted vice').
But according to Lovett, most of what befell women was their
own responsibility. Too often they were unfaithful to a proper
code of morality, as in their refusal to take the elementary pre-
caution of working in separate areas from men. Lovett, seemingly,
went the whole hog in his insistence that women conform to
prescriptive behaviour. In the process, he lost the cutting edge
of his radicalism.

His conversion to the economic tenets of political economy

also put Lovett at war with his former self. The radical reformer of the 1830s had expressed traditional working-class political attitudes. The moral reformer of the 1840s had urged balance, moderation, and the enjoyment of intellect and body. The late Lovett was a puritan whose writings contain numerous injunctions to resist the snares of the world. Working-class homes, he told his readers, must be 'convenient, cleanly, and tasteful, a scene of concord, love, and happiness, ... where children are trained up in knowledge and virtue'.[22] Clothing had to be discreet; otherwise it would become a 'flimsy folly, suited only for the fashionable hour, and then cast aside as useless'.[23] Always it was necessary to subordinate and control the moral impulses. The alternative was a deterioration in personal and social organisation which might lead ultimately to the destruction of nations.

Lovett, the newly-minted proponent of middle-class respectability and propriety, played an unobtrusive public role during the remaining years of his life. He moved farther away from the centre of London, although he continued to spend time in Clerkenwell and Bloomsbury. With the assistance of Ellis, he supported himself and his wife and daughter more comfortably than he had done in previous decades. And he worked industriously to advance causes he now adopted as his own. Temperance was one such cause. For many years Lovett worked for the UKA, a pressure group that favoured state control of licensing facilities. He was also active in the Land Tenure Reform Association, founded in 1869, and led by John Stuart Mill and George Howell. This organisation championed the abolition of primogeniture and the taxation of the unearned increment in land values, ideas presented in embryo by Ricardo earlier in the century and popularised by Henry George in the 1880s. Lovett's support for these land policies represented a fusion of his old radical beliefs with their hostility to the aristocracy and a revamped approach to questions of finance and administration. He also belonged to

the Anti-Game Law League, which agitated on this complementary issue linking old radicalism and new liberalism. And he
continued as often as he could to speak up for pacifism, as a
member of W. R. Cremer's Workmen's Peace Association,
formed in 1871, and as the author of essays in newspapers and
magazines. Repeatedly, as in a series of articles he wrote for the
Bee-Hive in 1868, Lovett called for a mechanism of international
arbitration – preferably a 'general court of judicature for all
nations' – to resolve disputes and avert wars.

Yet, in some ways Lovett's most interesting organisational
affiliation was with the National Sunday League, founded in 1855.
This group took up the old Lovett war cry of anti-sabbatarianism,
which he had formulated in his petitition of 1829. It agitated for
the opening of places of 'rational recreation' on Sundays, like
the Crystal Palace and the British Museum, in order that workingmen could spend the day productively engaged. The interesting thing about Lovett's connection with the NSL is that it
pointed up how conventional and 'middle-class' he had become
in his final years. His conception of self-improvement for the
poor was narrowly linked to moral channels, as was that of the
NSL. Like the NSL, Lovett condemned pleasures which he
deemed wasteful, especially gambling, smoking, and attendance
at music-halls. He distinguished more precisely than he had done
earlier between the usefully permissible (which anti-sabbatarian
legislation was intended to promote) and the merely enjoyable,
which might if uncontrolled lead to a life of dissolution and
decay. In the 1850s and 1860s anti-sabbatarianism had a moral
focus for Lovett: no longer did it mean freedom for its own sake
or as a way of asserting the claims of an oppressed class.

Lovett's writings during his final years are saturated with
political economy. They contain numerous references to Mill
(especially on the subject of land), Charles Babbage, Ricardo,
Bentham, and above all Ellis. In 1868, when Robert Hartwell, a

friend from Chartist days was managing the *Bee-Hive*, Lovett wrote two lengthy series of articles for the paper. One, entitled 'The ABC of Social Science', was a simplistic primer of political economy; the other was a more sophisticated melange of ideas about social problems entitled 'Memorandums for Future Reformers'. In the 'ABC of Social Science' Lovett advocated population control for the first time and made clear the link between capital accumulation as a way of increasing income and the cultivation of morality. He urged savings and labour as the chief instruments whereby the poor could elevate themselves to a better position in society: 'Men have a just and absolute right to every kind of property which they can fashion or create by the labour of their head or hands . . .'.[24] Employers who treat their workpeople like serfs and workmen who do not give 'a fair day's labour for a fair day's wages' are equally to blame for economic failure, although in Lovett's view the latter unfairly carried the brunt of the criticism. He likewise proposed taxes on land and income in place of the stultifying customs and excise duties.

The 'Memorandums for Future Reformers' contained a few ideas new to Lovett. These reflect an acceptance of state interference as a prop to personal effort. Thus he advocated loans to private contractors to encourage them to construct 'spacious, cheap, healthful and convenient homes for the people';[25] stringent legal punishments for the adulteration of food; and the elimination of 'poisonous air' and impure water to help make cities healthier places in which to live. In political matters he reiterated the case for an expanded suffrage (while abandoning his commitment to universal suffrage), the secret ballot, and equal electoral districts. But along with these claims he proffered an idea (further publicised in an 1869 pamphlet entitled *Proposals for Establishing a Cheap, Just and Efficient Mode of Electing Members of Parliament and for Securing the Just and Equal Representation of the Whole People*) that MPs should be chosen from competency lists based on public examinations.

It was necessary, he claimed, for politicians to have a working knowledge of basic subjects as well as an understanding of 'social and political principles of right and justice'. Only then could the Commons play its rightful, constitutional role and the aims of good legislation be carried out: to secure 'an efficient system of education, equal and just representation, cheap and effective government, perfect freedom of commerce, equal rights, freedom of opinion, and cheap law and justice for all classes'.[26]

Lovett died in Euston Road, London, on 8 August 1877 after a brief illness. Although he lived to the ripe age of seventy-seven, his life was dogged for many years by physical illnesses and a bodily 'sensitivity' that irritated some of his friends. Still, he was robust enough to fight for the causes he believed in up to the very end. His autobiography, in which he looked back triumphantly upon his major achievements, was completed and published a year before his death. Only a small number of mourners were present for his funeral at Highgate Cemetery. Moncure Conway, the deist minister of South Place Chapel, conducted the services. There were brief obituaries in papers like *The Times* and the *Examiner* but no outpouring of public tributes. Lovett was recollected as the man who had put Chartism on the political map and as a leader in the struggle for adult education. Perhaps Holyoake (whom he had treated badly in the 1840s) offered the most charitable judgement. Quoting W. R. Greg, he said of Lovett at his graveside: 'It is not by the monk in his cell, or the saint in his closet, but by the valiant worker in humble sphere and in dangerous days, that the landmarks of liberty are pushed forward.'[27]

The chief interest in Lovett's life is to try to relate his biography to events at large. It would make for a smooth ending to be able to interpret his life as a paradigm of the increasing 'moderation' of the working classes. Perhaps in some ways it was. Yet none of the general historical themes of the period fit Lovett particularly well. He was not a true labour aristocrat. He took little interest in cabinet-making and earned small sums from it. During the final thirty years of his life he was an educator and writer, not an artisan. Upward mobility does not reveal much about his shift from radicalism to liberalism. He did not earn enough to qualify for the franchise until the Reform Act of 1867 extended it to lodgers; his position at the end of his life was substantially the same as it had been at the beginning. He was poor, probably never earning on average more than £1 a week. The closest general links between Lovett and the working-class movement of the early and mid-Victorian years are probably to be found in the explanations of Brian Harrison and Trygve Tholfsen, which emphasise the adoption of common values by working and middle classes. Certainly the 'late' Lovett's obsessions with middle-class notions of respectability are connected with earlier stages of his life. His class feelings gave way to a commitment to self-improvement; this in turn led to the adoption of a more unattenuated brand of liberalism.

Yet it may be dangerous to assume an 'inevitability' in this. Lovett was an individual. He was a strong-willed and decisive leader of disaffected workingmen. His career went through three stages. Towards the end he began to parody himself, to the extent that he became almost too 'typical' of some of the shifts from left to right that were occurring in these decades. Some reformers followed similar paths, including Vincent and Lowery. But most did not. Who is to say what is typical? Lovett did not lead many workingmen into political economy with him. He cut himself off from the Chartist political tradition, perhaps too abruptly, and never managed to reconcile his class-consciousness with the middle-class outlook he championed at the end. By the time Lovett adopted Ellis as his mentor he had shed his popular radicalism. He could not juggle the two, and it may be argued that in this failure to synthesise both views he remained unfaithful to the earlier, more important phases of his life. It is probably best, therefore, to regard Lovett as an individual, not a type. He took and gave what he chose over a long and fruitful career, and more often than not resisted the influence of others.

Lovett has had a good press and is remembered in Newlyn where a plaque was erected in 1948 (on the centenary of the climax of the Chartist movement) and again in 1977 to commemorate his death. Certainly he had his faults. His temperament was defective to the extent that he sometimes allowed personal differences to shape his political commitments. He was often inconsistent. At times he had a private as well as a public agenda. He could be mean-spirited and crotchety. But he possessed an unusual measure of integrity and believed throughout his life in justice for the working classes. He fought hard to improve their lot, even towards the end when his convictions as to how this could best be accomplished had changed drastically. He possessed a zeal and enthusiasm that held up well in the face of many discouraging setbacks. He was a pioneer and a plodder where other reformers lacked the stamina to continue to pursue a better life. If Lovett was neither as great a man as some of his supporters contend nor as insignificant as several recent detractors maintain, he was nonetheless an unusual and outstanding reformer: one who made permanent contributions to working-class politics and education.

Notes

Introduction

1 M. Beer, *A History of British Socialism* (London: G. Bell and Sons, 1919-20), vol. II, p. 5.

2 R. H. Tawney, Introduction to *Life and Stuggles of William Lovett* (London: G. Bell and Sons, 1920), pp. xxi, xxiv.

3 Michael Foot, *Loyalists and Loners* (London: Collins, 1986), p. 254.

4 Brian Harrison, 'William Lovett and education', *History Today*, 37 (1987), p. 16.

Chapter 1

1 *Life and Struggles of William Lovett in His Pursuit of Bread, Knowledge, and Freedom* (London: Trübner and Co., 1876), p. 8.

2 *Ibid.*, p. 2.

3 *Ibid.*, p. 35.

4 *Magazine of Useful Knowledge*, 30 October 1830.

5 Quoted in J. F. C. Harrison, *Robert Owen and the Owenites in Britain and America: The Quest for the New Moral World* (London: Routledge and Kegan Paul, 1969), p. 48.

6 *Life and Struggles*, p. 43.

7 *Weekly Free Press*, 10 April 1830.

8 *Magazine of Useful Knowledge*, 10 October 1830.

9 *Proceedings of the Third Co-operative Congress Held in London, and Composed of Delegates from the Co-operative Societies of Great Britain and Ireland* (London: William Strange, 1832), p. 7.

10 *Ibid.*, p. 5.

Chapter 2

1 *Life and Struggles of William Lovett* (London: MacGibbon and Kee, 1967 edition), p. 55.

2 *Penny Papers for the People*, 27 May 1831.

3 *Life and Struggles*, 1967 ed., p. 59.

4 *Ibid.*

5 Lovett to Francis Place, 26 July 1835, Add. Ms. 27,791, Place Papers, British Library.

6 *Life and Struggles*, 1876 ed., p. 71.

7 Place Newspaper Collection, Set 63, Vol. I, British Library.

8 *Morning Chronicle*, 1 November 1831.

9 *A Political Register*, 28 January 1831.

10 *Poor Man's Guardian*, 17 September 1831.

11 *Ibid.*, 25 February 1832.

12 *Ibid.*

13 *Ibid.*, 11 February 1832.

14 *Middlesex Sessions, May 16th, 1832: A Correct Report of the Trial of Messrs. Benbow, Lovett, & Watson, as the Leaders of the Farce Day Procession* (London: James Watson, 1832), p. 20.

15 *Cleave's Weekly Police Gazette*, 13 February 1836.

16 *Life and Struggles*, 1876 ed., p. 59.

17 Place Newspaper Collection, Set 56, Vol. I.

18 *'Destructive', and Poor Man's Conservative*, 11 May 1833.

Chapter 3

1 D. J. Rowe, 'The London Working Men's Association and the "People's Charter"', *Past and Present*, no. 36 (1967), p. 79.

2 *Life and Struggles*, 1967 ed., p. 75.

3 *Ibid.*, 1876 ed., p. 92.

4 *Ibid.*, 1967 ed., p. 76.

5 *Address and Rules of the Working Men's Association, for Benefiting Politically, Socially and Morally the Useful Classes* (London: John Cleave, 1836), p. 3.

6 *The Rotten House of Commons, Being an Exposition of the Present State of the Franchise, and an Appeal to the Nation on the Course to be Pursued in the Approaching Crisis* (London: Henry Hetherington, 1836), p. 3.

7 *The Working Men's Association, to the Working Classes of Europe, and Especially to the Polish People* (London: John Cleave, 1838), p. 5.

8 *The Radical Reformers of England, Scotland, and Wales, to the Irish People* (1836), as quoted in *Life and Struggles*, 1876 ed., p. 193.

9 Lovett Collection, Vol. I, pp. 26-7, Birmingham Public Library.

10 From an address quoted in *Life and Struggles*, 1876 ed., p. 130.

11 Copies of the five letters (*Hetherington's Twopenny Dispatch*, 5-7/1836) are in Place Newspaper Collection, Set 56, Vol. I.
12 *Life and Struggles*, 1876 ed., pp. 445-6.
13 Lovett Collection, Vol. I, pp. 26-7.
14 Letter in *True Sun*, reprinted in *Poor Man's Guardian*, 30 August 1834.
15 Circular in Place Newspaper Collection, Set 52, f. 405.
16 *Ibid.*.
17 *Life and Struggles*, 1876 ed., p. 161.
18 James Epstein, *The Lion of Freedom: Feargus O'Connor and the Chartist Movement, 1832-1842* (London: Croom Helm, 1982), p. 51.
19 Lovett Collection, Vol. II, p. 242.
20 *Ibid.*.
21 Quoted in Place Papers, Add. Ms. 27,819, f. 358.

Chapter 4

1 Quoted in J. T. Ward, *Chartism* (London: B. T. Batsford, 1973), p. 104.
2 Lovett to Place, 11 March 1839, Place Papers, Add. Ms. 35,151, f. 147.
3 *Life and Struggles*, 1876 ed., p. 171.
4 *Ibid.*, p. 172.
5 National Association Gazette, 4 June 1842 (subsequently reprinted in *Brief Sketches of the Birmingham Conference By a Member* (London: 1842)).
6 Quoted in T. M. Parsinnen, 'Association, convention and anti-Parliament in British radical politics, 1771-1848', *English Historical Review*, LXXXVIII (1973), p. 522.
7 Add. Ms. 27,821, f. 56.
8 Place to Lovett, 13 March 1839, Lovett Collection, Vol. II, p. 319a.
9 *A Letter to Mr. William Lovett, Sometime Resident in Warwick Gaol* (London: Effingham Wilson, 1841), p. 6.
10 *Life and Struggles*, 1876 ed., p. 211.
11 Lovett Collection, Vol. II, p. 26.
12 *The Trial of W. Lovett, Journeyman Cabinet-maker, for a Seditious Libel, Before Mr. Justice Littledale, at the Assizes at Warwick, on Tuesday, the 6th August, 1839* (London: Henry Hetherington, 1839), p. 3.
13 Place Newspaper Collection, Set 55, f. 2.
14 William Lovett to Mary Lovett, 10 January 1839, Place Newspaper Collection, Set 55, f. 72.
15 Lovett to Place, 20 July 1840, Place Newspaper Collection, Set 55, f. 683.

Chapter 5

1 Lovett to Place, 22 June 1840, Place Newspaper Collection, Set 55, f. 602a.
2 News cutting from the *Northern Star*, in Place Newspaper Collection, Set 55, f. 700.
3 *Life and Struggles* 1876 edition, p. 138.
4 William Lovett and John Collins, *Chartism: A New Organisation of the People* (London: James Watson, 1840), p. 16.
5 *Ibid.*, p. 1.
6 *Ibid.*, p. 22
7 *Ibid.*, p. 47.
8 *Ibid.*, p. 53.
9 Introduction to 1920 edition of Lovett's *Life and Struggles* (London: G. Bell and Sons), Vol. I, p. xxviii.
10 *Northern Star*, 17 April 1841.
11 *National Association Gazette*, 9 April 1842.
12 *Ibid.*, 22 January 1842.
13 *Ibid.*, 29 January 1842.
14 Henry Richard, *Memories of Joseph Sturge* (London: S. W. Partridge, 1864), p. 301.
15 *Nonconformist*, 13 April 1842.
16 *Life and Struggles*, 1876 edition, p. 277.
17 *Ibid.*, p. 180.
18 *Nonconformist*, 28 December 1842.
19 *Birmingham Journal*, 31 December 1842, reprinted in G. D. H. Cole and A. W. Filson, *British Working Class Movements: Select Documents, 1789-1875* (London: Macmillan and Co., 1951), pp. 388-9.

Chapter 6

1 Harrison, 'Wiliam Lovett and education', p. 22.
2 Moore to Francis Place, 11 December 1841, Place Newspaper Collection, Set 55, f. 723.
3 Mill to Lovett, 27 July 1842, Lovett Collection, Vol. IV, p. 220.
4 National Association Minute Book, May 1843, Add. Ms. 37,774, British Library.
5 J. F. C. Harrison, *The Common People: A History from the Norman Conquest to the Present* (London: Croom Helm, 1984), p. 286.

6 *Life and Struggles*, 1876 edition, p. 229.

7 NA Minute Book, February 1846, Add. Ms. 37,775.

8 Lovett to William Lloyd Garrison, 1 March 1847, in *People's Paper*, 24 April 1847.

9 Lewis L. Lorwin, *Labour and Internationalism* (London: George Allen and Unwin, 1929), p. 17.

10 *Life and Struggles*. 1876 edition, p. 299.

11 *Address to the Friends of Humanity and Justice Among all Nations, by the Democratic Friends of all Nations* (London: John Cleave, 1845), pp. 4, 6.

12 *Address from the Members of the National Association . . . to the Working Classes of France, on the Subject of War* (London: C. H. Elt, 1844), pp. 4, 6.

13 *An Address from the National Association . . . to the Working Classes of America, on the War Spirit that is Sought to be Excited Between the Two Countries* (London: John Cleave, 1846), pp. 3, 5.

14 *Address to the French People* (1848), quoted in *Life and Struggles*, 1876 edition, p. 330.

15 *An Humble Apology for Peace, by the National Association, in Reply to 'An Humble Apology for War', which Appeared in the 'Liverpool Journal'* (London: C. H. Elt, 1844), p. 4.

16 *The Peace Principle, the Great Agent of Social and Political Progress: Being a Short Review of the Peace Doctrines of the 'Family Herald'* (London: Charles Gilpin, 1849, p. 7.

17 *The People's League, to the People of London and Its Vicinity* (London: Charles Fox, 1848), p. 6.

18 *Address to the Radical Reformers of the United Kingdom* (1848), quoted in *Life and Struggles*, 1876 edition, p. 338.

19 *Ibid.*.

20 *Ibid.*, p. 348.

Chapter 7

1 *Life and Struggles*, 1876 ed., p. 374.

2 *Ibid.*, p. 381.

3 William Lovett, *Elementary Anatomy and Physiology, for School and Private Instruction; with Lessons on Diet, Intoxicating Drinks, Tobacco, and Disease* (London: Darton & Co., 1851), p. xiv.

4 *Life and Struggles*, 1876 ed., p. 135.

5 William Lovett, *Social and Political Morality* (London: Simpkin, Marshall &

Co., 1853), p. 141.

6 *Life and Struggles*, 1876 ed., p. 57.

7 *Poor Man's Guardian*, 30 March 1833.

8 *Alliance News*, 16 April 1870.

9 *Ibid.*, 18 June 1870.

10 *English Chartist Circular*, Vol. II, pp. 29-30.

11 *National Association Gazette*, 23 April 1842.

12 *Social and Political Morality*, p. 21.

13 *Ibid.*, pp. 45-6.

14 *Ibid.*, p. 125.

15 *Ibid.*, p. 184.

16 *National Association Gazette*, 1 January 1842.

17 William Lovett, *Woman's Mission* (London: Simpkin, Marshall & Co., 1856), p. 8.

18 *Ibid.*, p. 10.

19 *Ibid.*, p. 14.

20 *Social and Political Morality*, p. 96.

21 *Alliance News*, 13 August 1870.

22 *Ibid.*, 9 July 1870.

23 *Social and Political Morality*, p. 96.

24 *Bee-Hive*, 23 May 1868.

25 *Ibid.*, 25 July 1868.

26 *Ibid.*, 20 June 1868.

27 George Jacob Holyoake, *Sixty Years of an Agitator's Life* (London: T. Fisher Unwin, 1892), Vol. II, p. 269.

Further reading

Lovett's *Life and Struggles* was published initially in 1876. A two-volume edition with a preface by R. H. Tawney was reprinted in 1920. Another edition was published in 1967 minus the final three chapters, which contain important information about Lovett's activities after 1848. As well as yielding valuable insight into Lovett's career as a reformer, *Life and Struggles* contains substantial excerpts from many of his tracts and pamphlets. These writings are otherwise generally inaccessible outside major repositories like the British Library, the Goldsmiths' Library of the University of London, and in particular the collection of Lovett material in the Birmingham Central Library, which includes letters to and from Lovett and the bulk of his published writings. Substantial manuscript material relevant to Lovett is also to be found in the Francis Place Papers and the Place Newspaper Collection in the British Library; the Home Office and secret service papers in the Public Record Office; and minutes of various organisations with which Lovett was connected, notably the London Working Men's Association, the Chartist Convention of 1839, and the National Association (all in the British Library).

Lovett was not a prolific writer but he wrote many tracts, some of which are listed below. He also contributed to many of the radical newspapers and periodicals of his day. Copies of these newspapers and periodicals are scattered in many libraries and once again the British Library is the best source. A sample of Lovett's more important published writings are listed below, along with a selection of secondary literature.

Books and pamphlets by Lovett

(not including the many tracts written by him for the various organisations to which he belonged)

Tyranny and Robbery in Support of the Militia Laws!!, Henry Hetherington, 1831.

Middlesex Sessions, May 16th, 1832: A Correct Report of the Trial of Messrs. Benbow, Lovett, and Watson, as the Leaders of the Farce Day Procession, James Watson, 1832.

The Eloquent and Patriotic Defence of William Lovett . . . on the 6th of August, 1839, for Alleged Libel and Sedition, James Guest, 1839.

(together with William Collins) *Chartism: A New Organization of the People,* James Watson, 1840, 1841; Leicester University Press, 1969 (with an introduction by Asa Briggs).

To the Political and Social Reformers of the United Kingdom, R. E. Lee, 1841.

A Letter to Daniel O'Connell, Esq., M.P. in Reply to the Calumnies He Put Forth in the Corn Exchange, August 8th . . . , Henry Hetherington, 1843.

Letter to Messrs. Donaldson and Mason: Containing His Reasons for Refusing to be Nominated Secretary of the National Chartist Association, London, 1843.

A Proposal for the Consideration of the Friends of Progress, John Cleave, 1847.

Justice Safer than Expediency: An Appeal to the Middle Classes on the Question of the Suffrage, C. H. Elt, 1848.

The Peace Principle, the Great Agent of Social and Political Progress, Charles Gilpin, 1849.

Elementary Anatomy and Physiology, Darton & Co., 1851.

Social and Political Morality, Simpkin, Marshall & Co., 1853.

Woman's Mission, Simpkin, Marshall & Co., 1856.

Proposals for Establishing a Cheap, Just, and Efficient Mode of Electing Members of Parliament . . . , London, 1869.

Further reading

The Life and Struggles of William Lovett in His Pursuit of Bread, Know-ledge, and Freedom . . . , Trübner & Co., 1876; G. Bell & Sons, 1920 (with an introduction by R. H. Tawney); MacGibbon & Kee, 1967 (minus the last three chapters).

Additional reading

John J. Beckerlegge, *William Lovett of Newlyn: The Cornish Social Reformer*, privately printed, 1948.

Max Beer, *A History of British Socialism*, 2 vols., G. Bell & Sons, 1919-20.

John Breuilly, 'Artisan economy, artisan politics, artisan ideology: the artisan contribution to the nineteenth-century European labour movement', in Clive Emsley and James Walvin (eds.), *Artisans, Peasants and Proletarians, 1760-1860*, Croom Helm, 1985.

G. D. H. Cole, *Chartist Portraits*, Macmillan, 1941 (includes an essay on Lovett).

James Epstein, *The Lion of Freedom: Feargus O'Connor and the Chartist Movement, 1832-1842*, Croom Helm, 1982.

Michael Foot, 'The Chartist William Lovett', in *Loyalists and Loners*, Collins, 1986.

David Goodway, *London Chartism, 1838-1848*, Cambridge University Press, 1982.

L. Barbara Hammond, *William Lovett, 1800-1877*, Fabian Society pamphlet, 1922.

Brian Harrison, 'William Lovett and education', *History Today*, 37 (1987), pp. 14-22.

J. F. C. Harrison, *Robert Owen and the Owenites in Britain and America: The Quest for the New Moral World*, Routledge & Kegan Paul, 1969.

Eric Hobsbawm and Joan Scott, 'Political shoemakers', in Hobsbawm, *Workers: Worlds of Labour*, Weidenfeld & Nicolson, 1984

Patricia Hollis, *The Pauper Press: A Study in Working-Class Radicalism of the 1830's,* Oxford University Press, 1970.

Mark Hovell, *The Chartist Movement*, ed. and completed by T. F. Tout, Manchester University Press, 1925.

David Large, 'William Lovett' in Patricia Hollis (ed.), *Pressure from Without in Victorian England,* Edward Arnold, 1974.

David Large, 'William Lovett', in *Dictionary of Labour Biography,* ed. John Saville and Joyce Bellamy, vol. 6, Macmillan Press, 1982.

T. M. Parsinnen, 'Association, convention and anti-Parliament in British radical politics, 1771-1848', *English Historical Review,* LXXXVIII (1973), pp. 504-33.

I. J. Prothero, 'Chartism in London', *Past and Present*, 44 (1969), pp. 76-105.

I. J. Prothero, *Artisans and Politics in Early Nineteenth Century London: John Gast and His Times*, Dawson, 1979.

D. J. Rowe, 'The London Working Men's Association and the 'People's Charter'', *Past and Present*, 36 (1967), pp. 73-86.

F. B. Smith, 'British Post Office espionage, 1844', *Historical Studies*, XIV (1970), pp. 189-203.

Trygve Tholfsen, *Working Class Radicalism in Mid-Victorian England,* Columbia University Press, 1977.

Dorothy Thompson, *The Chartists: Popular Politics in the Industrial Revolution,* Maurice Temple Smith, 1984.

E. P. Thompson, *The Making of the English Working Class,* Victor Gollancz, 1963.

Alex Tyrell, *Joseph Sturge and the Moral Radical Party in Early Victorian Britain,* Croom Helm, 1987.

Henry Weisser, *British Working-Class Movements and Europe, 1815-48,* Manchester University Press, 1975.

Henry Weisser, 'William Lovett', in *Biographical Dictionary of Modern British Radicals,* ed. Joseph O. Baylen and Norbert J. Gossman, vol. 2, Harvester Press, 1984.

Further reading

Joel H. Wiener, *The War of the Unstamped: The Movement to Repeal the British Newspaper Tax, 1830-1836,* Cornell University Press, 1969.

Joel H. Wiener, *Radicalism and Freethought in Nineteenth-Century Britain: The Life of Richard Carlile,* Greenwood Press, 1983.

Index

Index

Hartwell, Robert, 43-4, 56, 135-6
Hetherington, Henry, 10, 19-20, 22-3, 28-9, 31, 32, 38, 42, 43-4, 49, 56, 71, 73, 78, 85, 92, 98, 103, 104, 106, 115, 116, 125
Hibbert, Julian, 21, 60, 104
Hodgskin, Thomas, 15, 47
Holyoake, George Jacob, 104-6, 114, 116, 137
Howitt, William, 113-14
Hume, Joseph, 22, 28, 49, 86-7, 115, 116-17
Hunt, Henry, 6, 16, 19, 20, 22, 60, 76

internationalism, 46-7, 103-13, 130, 135

Linton, William James, 88, 96, 100, 110-11, 115
London Society of Cabinet-Makers, 8, 52
London Working Men's Association, 18, 32, 36-51, 60-1, 63, 65, 74-5, 81, 83, 84-5, 88, 97, 105, 107, 108-9, 124-5, 126, 131
Lovett, Mary, 8-9, 33, 60, 62, 73, 103, 132
Lowery, Robert, 62, 92, 96, 116, 125

Mazzini, Giuseppe, 47, 108-9, 110-11
Metropolitan Political Union, 22-3
Miall, Edward, 90-4, 111, 112, 115, 116, 128
militia service, 27-8, 112-13
Mill, John Stuart, 101, 129, 131, 132, 134, 135
Moore, Richard, 49, 78, 85, 99, 111, 123

National Association for the Political and Social Improvement of the People, 81, 83-4, 85-9, 96-113, 116, 119-21, 124-5, 126, 129-30, 131-2 *see also* National Hall
National Association Gazette, 89, 99, 105, 128, 132

National Charter Association, 37, 84-5, 87, 88, 91-4, 96
National Hall, 98-103, 110, 119-20, 124, 129
National Political Union, 26-7
National Sunday League, 135
National Union of the Working Classes, 23-8, 30-1, 41, 42, 58, 65
Neesom, Charles, 87, 106
Northern Star, 54, 61, 63, 84, 86-7

O'Brien, Bronterre, 49, 51, 60, 63, 66, 92, 115
O'Connell, Daniel, 22, 51, 53-5, 86-7
O'Connor, Feargus, 2, 6, 11, 36-7, 40, 41, 42-3, 51-6, 60, 61-2, 65, 66-8, 69, 74, 76, 79, 81, 84-8, 90-4, 96, 97, 106-7, 115
Owen, Robert, 12-13, 15, 17, 41, 52
Owenism, *see* economic co-operation

Paine, Thomas, 9, 24, 47, 65, 104, 106
parliamentary reform, 20-7, 44-5
Parry, John H., 88, 89, 111, 116, 118
peace movement, *see* internationalism
People's International League, 111
People's League, 116-17
Place, Francis, 22, 23, 25-6, 38-40, 47, 48-50, 51, 53-4, 56, 59, 65, 73, 75, 79-80, 106, 117, 118, 128
political reform, *see* parliamentary reform
poor law, 56, 64, 78-9, 85, 87, 107
Poor Man's Guardian, 23, 25, 26, 28-9, 31, 42

Radical Reform Association, 20-3
Roebuck, John Arthur, 48-50

Smiles, Samuel, 77
Stallwood, Edmund, 87
Stephens, Joseph Rayner, 56, 66, 69